Breathing
as
Spiritual
Practice

———————

"Will Johnson sounds a clarion call for integration to a fragmented world. Ever the quintessential body and breath awareness teacher, Johnson skillfully brings together the three monotheistic religions by way of a spiritual practice common to all. Interwoven with his own candid, sometimes poignant, personal experience, Johnson offers a message of hope to all of us, wherever we find ourselves in our desire to be present to what is."

ANTOINETTE VOÛTE ROEDER,
SPIRITUAL DIRECTOR, POET, AND AUTHOR OF
POEMS FOR MEDITATION AND *THE SPACE BETWEEN*

Breathing
as
Spiritual
Practice

*Experiencing
the Presence
of God*

Will Johnson

Inner Traditions
Rochester, Vermont

Inner Traditions
One Park Street
Rochester, Vermont 05767
www.InnerTraditions.com

Cataloging-in-Publication Data for this title is available from the
Library of Congress

ISBN 978-1-62055-687-0 (print)
ISBN 978-1-62055-688-7 (ebook)

Printed and bound in the United States by Versa Press, Inc.

10 9 8 7 6 5 4 3 2 1

Text design and layout by Priscilla Baker
This book was typeset in Garamond Premier Pro with Argent and Legacy Sans
used as display typefaces

To send correspondence to the author of this book, mail a first-class letter
to the author c/o Inner Traditions • Bear & Company, One Park Street,
Rochester, VT 05767, and we will forward the communication, or contact the
author directly at **www.embodiment.net**.

To the memory of my uncle, Lester Conner,
my first great teacher of the common ground
that binds all religions together as one.

*Blowing through heaven and earth, and in
our hearts and the heart of every living thing,
is a gigantic breath—a great Cry—
which we call God.*

NIKOS KATZANZAKIS,
REPORT TO GRECO

Contents

Introduction

Several years ago, while surveying the participants at a Buddhist meditation retreat I was teaching in Victoria, British Columbia, I became aware of something that struck me as unusual. In addition to what I playfully refer to as "the usual Buddhist suspects" who regularly attend my retreats—largely middle-class, educated, bighearted folks, most of whom had been raised as Christian, Muslim, or Jew but had left the fold of the religion of their birth to probe the interior space of their bodies and minds through Buddhist meditational practices—there were also a number of people from the Christian Contemplative Movement in attendance. This was new for me, and I found the presence of this group—and the suggestion of an intersection between belief and direct experience—both intriguing and exhilarating, if a bit puzzling at first.

Over the course of the retreat I came to understand that these folks, deeply and traditionally Christian in their faith and outlook, were—much like their Buddhist brothers and sisters—exploring breath as their primary vehicle for coming closer to a direct experience of what they used the word *God* to represent. Still very much drawn to the story and teachings of Christ, they had apparently become dissatisfied with faith and belief alone and wanted to experience God in a more visceral, direct way, and they spoke of how becoming more acutely aware of the eternal cycle of breath created in them glimmerings of the palpable, felt presence of God.

I very much enjoyed the participation of these people, and by the end of the retreat, I'd befriended an Anglican minister among them. A few weeks after the retreat ended, I went to visit him, and over coffee at a neighborhood shop, we dove into a fascinating conversation about the connection between God and breath.

"God is the breath of life," he would say. "God is what happens to you when you submit to your breath."

Although I've never couched my perceptions of the spiritual path in such overtly theistic language, I'd come to much the same conclusions over the many decades I've been practicing breath awareness from the Buddhist traditions. Becoming aware of the breath, and then surrendering to its impulse, the primal urgency to breathe, has always led me into a dimension of experience that feels so much richer, and frankly far more satisfying, than the more conventional condition of consciousness—primarily lost in thought and unaware of bodily presence and the cyclic motions of breath—that passes as normal in the world at large and from where I began my inquiry so many decades ago. I've mostly used terms like the Great Wide Open, the ground of being, the source of all things to describe the transformation that would occur. I have even, on occasion, echoed his words almost exactly through such statements as, "The Great Wide Open is what happens to you when you surrender completely to your breath." Call it what you will. Breath is the common denominator beneath the words, and breath has the ability to take you to the place that all the words—voiced so differently but so similar in intention—point directly to: the source, the ground state, the wide-open dimension, the God.

As we continued our conversation, I thought back to a passage from the Book of Genesis (2:7) that had always fascinated me as a child:

> *And the Lord God formed man of the dust of*
> *the ground, and breathed into his nostrils the*
> *breath of life, and man became a living being.*

Dust and breath. I remember as a child pondering the relationship between these two qualities that couldn't be more different from each other: the one visible and concrete, the other invisible and formless. Although we're made from the elements of Earth, we're also clearly different from the dust and particles of our planet and solar system. We live, we breathe, our hearts pound, blood courses through our veins, we strive to love and live and spend productive lives. Life comes from somewhere, and the explanation that God blew that life into us has always held a good deal of appeal to me, and this was especially true once I'd experienced in the world of Buddhist meditation how the initial awareness of the breath and the subsequent surrender to it can slowly, but radically, alter consciousness over time in a way that leaves me feeling so refreshed as to feel reborn.

As we spoke long into the afternoon, an idea took hold in my mind that this passage from the Old Testament was more than story, that it was not just an account of human creation but could be read as secret instruction for an esoteric breathing practice capable of taking us into the presence of God. Yes, God blew into Adam and brought him to life, but what about the breath I draw into my body right now? Am I breathing in the breath of God, recreating that seminal moment, that first breath, when humanity came alive through the grace of God's breath? Or something altogether different and compromised? And might there exist for every one of us the possibility to recreate that moment, to feel the presence of God blowing life into us, to bring the dynamic fullness of that presence directly into our body as lived experience in every breath we consciously take?

The reality, however, is that we don't breathe very deeply at all. We restrain our breath. We hold it back. We tense our bodies to form a kind of armoring wall that keeps the breath contained, shallow, held in. We take in just the amount of air we need for our body's physical survival but not enough to experience the felt presence of what I believe God to be. Clearly, if we're to recreate the original breath through which God created Adam, and to experience God's life-giving presence through that breath, we would need to relax the containment, soften the constrictions, and bring breath back to vibrant and dynamic life. By resisting our impulse to breathe deeply and fully, we resist the felt presence of God in our lives.

In the teaching I do in the Buddhist world, I have mostly focused on a single passage of instruction from the Satipatthana Sutta, a very early text whose words were supposedly spoken by the historical Buddha himself. This passage expresses the Buddha's culminating instructions on the awakening of the awareness of breath, and he tells us that *as you breathe in, breathe in through the whole body; as you breathe out, breathe out through the whole body.*

Now, every tenth-grade high school student who's ever successfully completed a course in human biology knows that we don't breathe through the whole body. We breathe through our nose and often our mouth as well, not through the whole body. The air we breathe goes only as far as the lungs, where it undergoes a transformation that, while it then does spread itself through the whole body, does so in a form that can no longer be viewed or understood as breath.

But the Buddha knew nothing about oxygen in the air and the exchange of gases in the lungs. He wasn't speaking of what we now view as anatomical fact. He was pointing to spiritual reality and a strategy by which you can alter your consciousness through experiencing breath come so alive that it can be felt to stimulate sensation in every little part of the body. With this understanding, the notion of breathing God into your body with every inhalation you take sounded like a reasonable theistic possibility. Even though the Buddha never embraced the concept of God, the experience he was pointing to, and the shift in consciousness that it requires and elicits, amounts to much the same thing.

So much of our chronic discomfort comes from turning

our back on our highest potential, sheepishly holding ourselves back from stepping out from the herd into the fullness of our life. We're like caged animals who've been kept captive for so long that they've forgotten that the door to their cage has actually always been open. If the winds of breath, the agent of the healing power of God, might have the power literally to blow away the pain and suffering we so often feel in our body, our mind, our emotions, why not surrender to its highest potential?

———◄►———

The Old Testament is one of the earliest books that binds us all together as a human species before the divisions and enmity of religion began to raise their tragic, and sometimes downright ugly, heads. The primary text of the Jewish people, the Old Testament, introduces us to the patriarch Abraham, but it's not just Jews who claim and celebrate him. Christians look to Abraham as the seminal founder of a lineage that would mature into the extraordinary personage of Jesus. And Muslims, too, look to the Old Testament and to the patriarch Abraham as a germinal figure whose teachings would eventually ripen into the revelations of the Prophet Muhammad. How is it possible that these three great religions, all of whom look to and claim the same figure as the founder of their faiths, behave so badly toward one another? And like brothers and sisters who squabble and bicker and fight among themselves and make everyone around them crazy in the process, I started to think of Christianity, Judaism, and Islam as the sibling rivals of the Abrahamic faith, which expressed belief in one all-consuming and pervasive presence, which each of these religions refers to as God. From Abraham comes our understanding of the unified substratum of which everything is an integral part and out of which everything was originally brought into being. Directly from Abraham comes the notion of the one, not the many. In spite of this commonality, however, each of the religions behaves like a child fighting for the mantle of his father, viewing itself as the sole, legitimate heir, denying its siblings any say or rights in the matter.

Suddenly, the passage from Genesis began to take on a whole different and larger implication. The notion of honoring scripture through breathing God in every inhalation you take, the action of moving beyond faith and belief into a direct experience of God's felt presence in each and every cell of your body, was not just something for a Jew to explore, for a Christian to practice, for a Muslim to enter into. It was for everyone. And if a Jew were to experience a transformation of his or her own body and mind into the felt presence of God, and so were a Christian and a Muslim, how could there possibly be any difference between what they were feeling and how could there possibly remain any enmity among the three? The siblings would have to put down their differences and embrace one another as brothers and sisters of the one same God. Underneath the competing stories is the life-giving current that edits out the superficial differences and speaks of this shared heritage through the language not of words but of felt experience.

So I decided that the next time I went into retreat, I'd take the theistic orientation of this practice with me and explore it as deeply as I possibly could. How can I breathe God into my body, into my being, on every breath I take? And what will release itself on the accompanying exhalation? If I give myself permission to look on breath as not just sustaining the life of my body, but as opening me to a direct experience of the presence of God, what will that breath have to be like, and what will I have to do to allow such a transforming breath to occur? This book is a journal, as faithful as possible an accounting of what happened to me and, more importantly, what might happen to you if you could give yourself a few days of your life to experience breathing and being breathed by God. Sometimes the entries into my journal read like instructions, other times observations, sometimes thought streams, other times like little poems. The feeling presence of God is always with us, but more often than not it's like the psychic itch of a phantom limb that we've cut off from ourselves. It's my intention in this book to show how that limb can be restored and reattached, indeed to show that it's always been here.

My uncle Lester, to whom this book is dedicated, preached to me from an early age the gospel of ecumenism. "All religions, all paths of spiritual endeavor, lead ultimately to the same goal, union with the one and same God, or whatever word you wish to use to describe the ultimate source from which everything springs. No religion is any better or truer than another. They're all just different attempts to make sense of it all, of how there can be so many billions of people and stars, but how everything is still connected to a single underlying source."

He was certainly a great lover of words. He devoted his life to the study of the Irish poet William Butler Yeats and taught at universities in both the United States and Ireland. During his summers he would travel to Sligo, Ireland, where he ran a school whose sole purpose was the immersed study and enjoyment of the profoundly mystical poetry of Yeats. Like me he'd been born a Jew, but in one intensely cathartic moment in his twenties he had converted to Catholicism and held true to that religion for the rest of his life.

"What happened?" I would ask him. "Why did you decide to leave the religion of your birth and embrace the Christian faith?"

"Well, for starters," he would tell me, "remember that one isn't any better or worse than the other. But for me it wasn't so much a choice I made but a choice that was made for me." He would go on to tell me about his service during World War II. It was a terrible time, he would say, and he hoped in his deepest heart that I would never have to be drawn into what he would describe as "man's worst aptitudes." He'd been part of the Allied Army that had crossed the English Channel on D-Day, June 6, 1944, and his unit had slowly begun advancing across France toward Germany. One day, while resting with his company in a large tent outside a French village, he'd suddenly felt an urgency to walk into and explore the town. "We were all exhausted," he would recount, "but still something in me drew me off my cot, laced up my boots, and off I went, in search of what I had no idea." When he got to the center of the town, he felt inexplicably drawn to the Catholic church, quite badly damaged from the ravages of the conflict but still somehow standing tall amid the rubble. He decided to enter the church, and at the very moment he walked through the doors and gazed at the colored windows and the austere figure of the crucified Jesus, he heard an enormous explosion that came from the direction of his regiment. He ran out the door and back to his tent and company only to find that a munitions cache had exploded very near the compound where all his companions lay resting. There were serious injuries and even deaths. "What would you have done, Will, had that been your experience? I became a Catholic on the spot, and its story continues to save and nourish me."

As the years go by and my body gets ever older, I sometimes think of myself as a kind of a poster child (well, all right, a poster elder) for the spirit of ecumenism. Born a Jew, but with a number of my mother's family converts to Catholicism, I teach in the Buddhist and Sufi worlds. As far as religions go, I have them all fairly well covered. They're each a part of me, and I love the truths that all of them, in their own way, express and represent. I don't feel more one than the other.

Uncle Lester would not infrequently engage me in conversations about religion. "Choose the one you feel the most at home in but know that they're all pointing in an identical direction." He would also express his sadness at the horrific history of conflict among the major religions. "So foolish. So sad. Like best friends who love each other, fighting amongst themselves for no good reason. So choose one over the others if it feels right to you. In my case, the choice was made for me. Maybe it'll be made for you, maybe it won't. But know this: at heart you're either all of them or none of them."

I've always liked that. If I'm one of them, I'm all of them, even though I may be viewing my life at any given moment more through one of their doctrinal lenses than the others'. Beneath the stories we were born to and largely identify ourselves with lie the body and the breath, our body formed from the common elements of Earth, our breath shared with everyone on the planet. Beneath the stories is the common source from which all the stories originally sprung. There may be a Jewish story, a Christian gospel, a Muslim narrative, but there isn't a Jewish breath distinct from a Christian breath different from a Muslim breath. The elements of Earth and the air we breathe are our common heritage, not the subsequent tales that divide us into tribes that view "the other" as threatening. The practice of Breathing God is for all those devout Christians, Muslims, and Jews (and for everyone else as well) for whom rites and rituals, systems of faith and belief, are not in themselves enough to satisfy their spiritual hunger, but who thirst for something more, something more direct and immediate, who long to experience firsthand, indeed, first body, the felt presence of God.

Abiquiu, New Mexico

God in the Desert

I could have sworn that the jackrabbit winked at me. He was just outside my window when I woke this morning to the first stirrings of life in the desert—the soft whistle of wind weaving down the canyon, the tentative conversations of the waking birds, the rising and falling pitch of the cicada's song, the gradual lightening of the deep indigo sky with its hints of coral, pink, mauve. I looked out my window, and there was the jackrabbit, looking right back up at me. Eye to eye. It almost seemed as though he were checking me out somehow, that he was as curious to know who might be occupying the small room I'd been given to live in for the next ten days as I was to see him. This was his world, after all, not mine, and I felt grateful toward him for allowing me to share it. Still, when he went and winked, it was a bit unsettling, my first experience of the alteration of normalcy that is reputationally normal for the desert. Then he turned away and shuffled out of sight. Hmmm. That was strange too, I thought. He didn't hop. He shuffled.

I'm in a small room, perhaps eight feet by ten feet, enough space for a single bed, a side table and lamp, a desk and chair, a primitively built wardrobe for my clothes, a door and a window. On the floor is a thick Navajo throw rug in tones of gray and brown. Hanging on the wall over the desk is a large reproduction of the famous Velazquez painting of the crucified Christ, also in somber grays and browns, whose stark imagery startled me when I saw it for the first time but whose extraordinary artistry I was coming to love and—strange to say for such an unflinchingly austere and tragic image—delight in.

My room is in an L-shaped adobe guesthouse at Christ in the Desert Monastery, the most remote monastery in the Western Hemisphere, tucked away at the end of a thirteen-mile dirt road in the Chama Canyon of northwestern New Mexico. The monastery is run by the Benedictines and is home and place of worship for about fifty monks of their order. The brothers of the order hail from every continent and are all dressed in black cloaks that allow them to cover their heads or leave them exposed, depending on the moment of the day or the need to be in undisturbed contemplation. The cloaked hood is like a "do not disturb" sign for their fellow monks, time to be or wrestle with themselves, time to be or wrestle with God. I knew that over the course of the next ten days, my respect for their silent and mindful presence and for their committed faith and belief in a story that they resonated so deeply with you'd think it had occurred recently, not two thousand years ago, would continue to grow.

To support my efforts in the retreat I was about to undertake, I had two requirements. The first was to do it at a residence of one of the three great major Western religions, and the Benedictine brothers—who treat everyone as a manifestation of Christ himself—couldn't have been more accommodating and welcoming to me, even though I wanted to use my time at their monastery to explore an esoteric interpretation of a breathing practice that, while I personally trace it to God's creative action in the Old Testament, was outside their prescribed rules of worship and spiritual observance.

The second requirement was to enter into retreat somewhere in the desert. All three of the great religions took form, were shaped and molded, marinated, baked, and brought to fruition in desert landscapes, and I wanted the exploration I was about to undertake to occur under similar circumstances, far from the crowded bustle and commerce of a city center, removed as far as possible from the routines of daily life that fill our schedules to overfull, away from the traffic and freeways and horns and noise that all too easily make it hard just to be with ourselves. The desert is silent and the desert is hot, and I have always felt that both heat and silence are important ingredients in the psychic stew in which Judaism, Christianity, and Islam were born and brewed. It was in the desert that each of these religions had found their God.

> *god cannot be known*
> *through the language of thought*
> *god can only be approached*
> *through the language of silence*
> *and silence speaks*
> *in the vocabulary of felt presence*
>
> *god's form takes its shape*
> *in all the physical objects*

and events in the universe
god's invisible essence is to be found
in the silent felt presence
that pervades the billions of forms
and ties them forever together
into a single piece

in the center of your center
permeating your entire body
is a silent feeling presence
and this felt presence is your link
your connection
your avenue into the garden of god's
    presence

Where better to encounter this silent presence than in a landscape of silence, with little or no intrusion from the jarring noises of the machines of human invention? The silence of the desert is as much felt as heard. You feel it as a physical presence as much as hear it as a quality of sound. It's an enormous, felt force and—because it's so absent of the noises of modern life—a distraction-free zone. In a landscape of solitude and silence, there's nothing to draw you out of yourself, to divert your attention away from focusing single-mindedly on breath, on sensations, on God.

to call silence
a quality of sound
is problematic

it's the absence of sound
but still you hear it
still you feel it

Furthermore, silence is a relative term at best. Although there are virtually no man-made sounds I can hear, as I leave my room for an early walk outside the guesthouse's grounds I am continually serenaded by the flowing river, the tittering birds, the scuttering feet of the rabbits, the crashing cymbals of thunder, and the showers of rain that follow. And even though the desert canyon presents itself as pristinely silent, with only the sounds of nature punctuating that silence, I am not. The first thing I notice on waking in the morning, after my jackrabbit friend, is how very noisy my mind is, thoughts thinking themselves, constantly yammering on about things that had little immediate relevance, constantly distracting me from feeling and hearing the ocean of silence that surrounded me. Strangely, in the city I don't hear this monologue inside my head so clearly as I do in the desert. It's as though the sounds of the cars and the scurrying people and the subways and the sirens of modern life drown out the litany of random, unbidden thoughts that constantly cover over the silent presence at my center. One of my hopes for the breathing practice I was about to undertake was that it might silence the thoughts, pull the plug on them, wash and drain them away, like water in a bath, so that only the emptiness of felt presence, of God, would remain.

Perched quietly atop a rock in the desert, opening my hearing to let the silent sound of the desert enter my ears,

I also become aware of another source of sound that's completely blocked out by the cacophony of city life. Inside my own body I become aware of the constant beat . . . beat . . . beating of my heart, a whooshing sound that must be blood being pumped through my veins, and a high-pitched frequency and buzzing, like the rising and falling melodies of nighttime cicadas and crickets, in my head. But at least these sounds are natural sounds, and I welcome them into the symphony of silent presence that the desert is constantly composing on the spot.

As I walk over to breakfast later in the morning, I already hear God speaking to me from the silence in the whistle and warble of the wind that flies past my ears, like some unseen spirit wanting to let me know of its presence in this valley. Is not the wind the breath of the desert?

———————

I knew that, many years before, the American artist Georgia O'Keeffe withdrew to the little town of Abiquiu in northwestern New Mexico, near the high desert canyon where the Christ in the Desert Monastery is situated—attracted no doubt, at least in part, to the pervasive silence that caused her creative process little distraction. What I hadn't counted on, however, was that this was no desert of barren rock and sand. In fact, it couldn't have been further from that. This desert was stunningly gorgeous, rich in color, more like a Maxfield Parrish painting of a southwestern version of the Garden of Eden than the desert that Moses labored in for over forty years to bring his people to a better place, the wasted hills in which Jesus battled his tormentors, the desolate mountaintop that Muhammad visited on a regular basis to hear from his angel.

The monastery is nestled up against sheer rock walls, hundreds of feet high, in shades of red, coral, and terra cotta with striated veins of ochers and soft grays, and these colors shift and modulate throughout the day depending on the positioning of the sun and the presence, or absence, of the moving clouds. It looks out over a valley that must have left the early Dust Bowl settlers from Oklahoma speechless, believing they'd come upon the Promised Land they were hoping to find or died and gone to heaven. Where the mountainous walls of the valley are not so steep, small green piñon and juniper trees dot the angled earth, growing out of the rocky soil, their roots giving stability to the ground that, in turn, stabilizes them. Flowers of yellow, soft lavender, and coral and the otherworldly arms and legs of ocotillo cactus are everywhere on the flatter ground. And through this fairyland of fertile earth, colored rock, and shifting sky runs the Rio Chama, which is the reason that this desert canyon sprouts so much green life.

Breathtaking beauty aside, however, it is still the desert, and the heat even of a September afternoon is enough to bake you dry . . .

> *the desert*
> *whether beautiful or barren*
> *bakes you*

but this intense dry heat
as challenging as it is
can also heal you

the heat of the desert
causes impurities in your body
   and mind
your lusts and angers
your feverish wantings and
   aversions
everything that keeps you from
   falling into god's embrace
to rise to the surface
where they can be exposed and
   discarded
not unlike how butter gets
   turned into ghee

the heat of the desert
transforms the butter of your
   psyche
into the ghee of your soul

once your soul feels the sweet
   warmth of god caressing it
you'll be hard pressed
to ever again feel satisfied
with the butter of your
   psyche

. . . and I sense, and hope, that the Chama Canyon is going to bake me, heating away whatever impurities of mind and spirit keep me from feeling union with God, as I begin my practice of opening myself to presence with every breath I am able consciously to take. Breathing in . . . breathing out . . . breathing in . . . breathing out. That's what I've come here to do.

———◄►———

To engage the practice of Breathing God, we first have to become aware of the breath, and even though breath is with us every moment of our lives, we take it so for granted that we're rarely ever aware of its constant, cyclical phases of breathing in, breathing out. Could not the same be said of God, who's with us every moment of our lives, but whom we take so for granted and whose presence we're so rarely ever aware of? Becoming aware of the breath is to begin the journey back to becoming aware of the presence of God.

And so I'm setting aside the first day simply to reacquaint myself with this most fundamental human act. I breathe in, and I breathe out. I don't try to change or alter the breath in any way. I don't try to make it fuller or larger or breathe in such a way that my mind might think I should be breathing. I just let the breath be as it is, and I let myself watch, and I do my best to make the billowing motions of the breath—breathing in, breathing out—the primary focus of my attention.

It doesn't matter what I'm doing. What matters is remaining, as best I possibly can, aware of every breath I take, my breath going in, my breath going out, throughout the entire day, whether I'm sitting, lying down, walking, eating, abluting, praying, meditating.

I do my best to become aware of the very first breath I take upon coming out of sleep and waking up . . .

There it is! Good morning, breath. Forgive me for forgetting and overlooking you. You've always been there for me even though I've been so neglectful of you.

. . . and I set the intention to remain as aware as I possibly can of every breath I take today.

But as soon as I look out the window and am startled by the rabbit, that awareness is gone. For all I know, I might as well not even be breathing. And, of course, I still am, but I am back to breathing *normally. Normal* is not at all necessarily *natural* as it's far more normal for us to be unnatural when it comes to the breath, more normal to restrain the breath, to hold back on it, to deny the natural expression of its potency.

What I observe, when I give myself permission to be honest about what this more normal pattern of breath is actually like, is that, when I'm not aware of my breath, I go off in a thought and tighten and tense my body, especially around my rib cage and upper belly. And then, when I go back to my breath, the thought tends to dissipate and the body relaxes more. Back and forth. All day long. Sometimes remembering the breath. Just as often forgetting about it completely and getting lost in thought and tense in body. Thousands of times a day remembering, then forgetting, then remembering to remember again.

Settling into my breath, I become progressively more sensitive to the sounds of nature—the birds, the winds, the shuffling animals of the ground—and the vast underlying silence that they embellish. Strangely, the silence can drown out the inner monologue of the mind one moment and make me acutely aware of it the next. The silence relaxes the body, even if only momentarily. At times I feel bored silly. At other times I get glimpses of what I think might happen when I surrender my body and mind to God. Sometimes I don't like what my body is feeling, what sensations are coming to the surface, being revealed, through this constant focusing and refocusing on the incessant binary dance of the breath moving in and out. Sometimes I want to give up, quit this nonsense. Sometimes I feel overwhelmed with the joy of being able to do nothing but follow my breath in this desert paradise.

> *awareness of breath*
> *is the foundation of the practice*
> *breathing in*
> *breathing out*
> *let me remain*
> *as aware as I possibly can*
> *of every breath I take today*

Foundational Breathing
the easiest way to do this
is to put your awareness
in your belly
feel the belly expanding and contracting

rising and falling
getting larger
getting smaller
with every breath you take
expanding on the inhalation,
retracting on the exhalation
breathing in
breathing out

in your lower torso
is a place of stability
a place that keeps your awareness
tethered to your breath
a place where distracting thought
can't so easily find you

By bringing the action of breath to consciousness, we more firmly root ourselves in the mystery of the present moment. The felt presence of God can only be experienced in the present, in this very moment, not the one that's just passed or the one yet to come, but in this moment only. Breath, too, only happens right now. The breath of yesterday is a memory, the breath of tomorrow but a thought of the future. The breath you breathe right now, this very one, in this very moment, is what can ground you in the life-giving presence of God. When we take our breath so for granted that we pay it little, if any, attention, we tend to go off on flights of thought. As interesting as these excursions may be, they take us away from presence. Breath brings us back down to Earth and grounds us in the sacred space and time of the present moment.

The present moment is the one holy moment through which God's presence stands a chance of being directly felt. It's a crack in the fabric of time between everything that's come before and everything that's yet to be, and through this crack the light and presence of God can break through the veils and touch us. Thoughts in the mind have the ability to obscure the sacred nature of God's presence. So as best you can, let go of your attachments to the thoughts in your mind, and your subsequent identification with them, and let thought come and pass through you like wind through the leaves of a tree. Thoughts clutter the space of the head like debris that accumulates at a bend in a river and impedes the river's flow. When you can let go of your identification with thoughts, your head becomes an open space, and it's in such an open space that God can enter. Breathing in, breathing out.

It's been a good first day. As my body gets into bed and invites sleep, I remain aware of my breath going in, my breath going out, breathing in . . . breathing out . . . until . . . that moment comes when I'm no longer aware of anything.

In Spiritu

I wake up early to the lightening of sky and the first tentative conversations of birds. So quiet. So still. The silence of stillness. No wind. The sun is still far behind the mesa wall that hovers above the guesthouse, so only a faint glow of light covers over the valley in front of me. After shedding the dream I was having . . .

I'm a passenger in a car. A young prince is driving the car. We stop on a dark street and walk up to an apartment. There's a party, but everyone leaves. I'm alone and wandering through the streets. How to get home? I'm in university; it's my senior year. I have to write a senior thesis, but it's already after Christmas, and I haven't started yet, and I don't even know what to write about, and suddenly winter has passed, and I haven't yet started, and it's no longer possible to finish what I haven't even been able to start.

. . . I remember my breath and turn my attention to it. Nothing is more important to me at this moment in time than to just watch and feel my breath breathing me in, breathing me out, breathing . . . breathing. An hour later the sun is up.

I get up and go to the window hoping that the rabbit will be there again. I look out and take a quick survey of the desert. Cactus, small trees, a scattering of flowers, the canyon walls in the distance; no rabbit. The morning desert, before the heat of the sun dilutes the brilliance of its palette, is the color of Navajo jewelry. Turquoise skies. Ocher sand. Silvery glints of light reflected off the river in the distance. I turn my attention back to my breath but start to feel a strange sadness that the rabbit's not there.

I lie back down in my bed . . . breathing . . . breathing. I stay with my breath but open my eyes and look around the room. Something's changed in the one day I've been here doing my best to stay aware of my breath. I don't quite know how to say this, but it looks a bit less . . . real . . . than it did when I first arrived two nights ago. Ordinarily, I hook my attention onto the world I look out on, and my breath just follows along without my even knowing. Today, it feels like foreground and background are trading places. The desk, dresser, chair, and rug, the visual objects of my little world, are fading away, receding. They don't look so solid, so substantial, so oomphy, so . . . real. Immersed in breath, the focal center of my attention shifts from the world I look out onto to the breath I feel into. Breath is my center, my focal point, the space in which I'm living my life right now. The world that surrounds me is receding, receding, more of a background dream than the main event. When I look out from the perspective of my breath, the world just looks different.

I remember the Buddha saying somewhere that the world of visual appearances is like a dream or a phantom. Could this be what he meant, that when we focus our awareness so narrowly onto our breath, when we climb inside it and realize we want to stay there, the world outside ourselves fades away, starts actually dissolving, and is shown to be more a dream that we create than a reality we're born into? Is our belief in the substantiality of this world itself an impediment to our passing through its veils and joining ourselves back to the creator of this world? Is God the Master Programmer, the ultimately clever video game maker, who's created a world that looks unbelievably convincingly real? Is the world a kind of holographic video game, and we win the game once we figure out how to dissolve the apparent reality of its appearances, pass through the crack in its façade, and move onto a whole new level where we become one with God again? Are there levels beyond union with God that I don't even know about?

I go back to my breath. Breathing in . . . breathing out . . . breathing in . . . again . . . again . . . aga . . . I feel a wave of sadness spreading over me, a fog of darkness, and it's not just the rabbit:

My mind's jumpy as a rabbit, and I really wish he'd come back. It's weird, but I miss him: I'm a small boy who had a toy taken away. I'm crying, then I get angry, really angry, crying-out angry. I remember someone I once cared for and liked who hurt me, and I feel angry. I didn't want to lose him as a friend. I feel anger at the politicians who represent everything my soul abhors. I have doubts that what I'm doing here at the monastery is going to give my soul what it so wants. I feel unworthy of the Benedictine brothers at this monastery . . . so mindful, so silent, so present, so accepting

*. . . acceptance. . . . acceptance. . . . Let go of the neurotic habit of judging.
Acceptance is healing's doorway someplace deep within, inside my body.
Yes, inside my body is where I need to go to heal. It's where my breath is. I
want to find my breath, my breath, my breath . . .*

. . . and on and on, in and out of awareness, back and forth
between being present in breath and lost in thought.

> *my prayer to myself*
> *my prayer of breath*
> *let me remember to remember*
> *to choose breath over thought*
>
> *as my mind caroms off*
> *into unbidden thoughts*
> *my attention is diverted*
> *not only from my breath*
> *but from god*
>
> *so be it*
> *as many times*
> *as i get lost in thought*
> *that's how many times*
> *i hope to remember to remember*
> *my breath*
> *my prayer to myself*

Even at a monastery where people go to withdraw from
the world to focus their attention on God, there's no end of

opportunities to go off on fantasy flights of pride and prejudice, irritation and longing, constant assessments of judgment. All too often, in spite of my best efforts to stay focused on the breath, my mind is caught up in a moment-by-moment commentary of critical thought as I start inevitably to survey the other guests and residents:

Will you just look at that bumbler? Look how high he goes and piles food on his plate and then takes a second helping, just as big. Maybe he's not well, has a worm. What interesting moccasins that guest is wearing. But what awful overpowering perfume her friend has on. Doesn't she realize that the aroma of the desert is fragrance enough? Could the guy in the room next to mine please stop his constant shuffling? Look at the layers of designer clothing and the multiple strands of jewels on this other person who's just shown up this Sunday morning to partake of Holy Communion. The clothing hangs, the jewelry drips. She must be a wealthy patron from Santa Fe. I don't like that the elder monks kow-tow to her. Some of the monks don't seem so much calm as exhausted. That one looks like a hobbit; the other with alopecia is so bright and joyful. The other brother stands and walks so tall and graceful, a cross between a Calvin Klein model and an NFL wide receiver . . .

It's not uncommon to go on a personal retreat hoping for peace and a silencing of mind, but what you so often get instead, or at least at first, is a megaphone amplifying the troubling voices inside your head. Breath is like a torch or flashlight that penetrates the recessed corners of our mind, revealing all the attitudes and impulses we do our best at never letting see the light of day. Submerged and hidden way down deep, we can fool ourselves into believing they don't exist. But through the illumination of the breath, these private pettinesses get dredged up and brought into open view where we can flee from them; stuff them back down to a place where we don't have to feel them, a place underneath our breath; . . . or be courageous enough to let them be, breathing into, not away from, them so they can let go the hold they have on us. Breathing in fully, breathing out just as deeply, all these dark creatures, these hidden parts of ourselves, start crawling out of the shadows of the woods and into the light—and there's not just one but all sorts of them.

I do my best to keep my attention focused on my breath, but all too often, all too easily, I lose that awareness as my mind in a kind of daydream, not all that different from my night dreams, takes off on excursions of thought mostly reliving events from my past, some of them happy, most of them not at all; sometimes looking forward to things to come, some of them happy, many less so. This constant obsession especially with the past, mentally reliving the trauma and disappointments, even the moments of victory, is what I call doing laps in the garbage dump of the past:

I know it's a bad swimming hole: the water brackish at best, polluted at worst, sharp rocks and scary predatory animals lurking not too far down. Yet the attraction is evidently irresistible. Don't fool yourself into thinking you're somehow above all this, but also don't shame yourself for losing your breath to these thoughts, for feeling things you don't want to feel, or thinking that you're not doing the practice right, or that you're not a suitable candidate for this journey of Breathing God. Remember that everything's OK, everything's OK. The practice is supposed to dredge up the sleepy detritus of the psyche . . . your sadnesses, your guilts, your angers, your fears, your so frequently unbidden thoughts exposing their story lines to the heat and light of wakefulness. The practice is supposed to show you just how much of the time you're lost in story lines of thought. Just keep breathing, go back to breathing, be aware of whatever your breath divulges, and let it be with the knowledge that shining light on shadows eventually dissolves them . . .

It honestly doesn't seem like a big ask. Just watching the breath, nothing but breath, these first few days, breathing in, breathing out, no longer oblivious to this most primal of human actions just because we keep breathing, whether we're aware of it or not. How can something so simple be so difficult and challenging? My mind doesn't want me to do this because the longer I'm able to sustain an unbroken awareness of breath the more I have to face unbidden thoughts, my catalog of shortcomings and foibles, my tendency to always make assessments in whatever company I keep as to where I stand on the pecking order of life, my irritations, my impatiences, my irks, my longings, my wild fantasies of revenge. Lurching down memory lane just takes me away from breath, from God. So humbling. Just being aware of breath coming in . . . breath going out . . . hard to do for more than a few seconds at a time before thoughts come rushing back in. Not only do they distract me from my breath, they can be petty, disturbing, boring, nasty, and frankly stupid, but the good news gospel here is that I can always remember to remember . . . once again . . . my breath.

Correlating breath with the felt presence of God is not an original idea. Jews speak of *ruach*, which can be thought of as wind, as spirit, as breath. When the Old Testament speaks of God as a spirit or wind that moves across the waters, stirring life into motion, that spirit is *ruach Elohim*, and when God blows the breath of life into Adam, that breath is also ruach. The Holy Spirit is *ruach hakodesh,* with clear implications that the life-giving spirit in humans is related to the breath and somehow dependent on it as well. The practice of Breathing God is a practice of ruach, for on every inhalation we take, we also connect with spirit, the felt presence of God, like a wind that blows itself directly into and through our bodies.

The Greek Orthodox Church speaks of *pneuma,* which again can be translated as wind, spirit, or breath. The term originates in ancient Greek medicine where pneuma was viewed as the circulating air necessary for the vital organs to function and for life to exist at all. It's also seen as the medium that sustains consciousness in a body and through which we can commune directly with God. In the Greek version of the New Testament, the word *pneuma* appears as often as does ruach in the Old Testament, and they are fundamentally identical, both referring to a life-giving breath that can elevate us, making us more buoyant in spirit, uplifted, floating, more one with God. In the present-day world, our cars ride on pneumatic tires filled with air that buoy the chassis and allow us seemingly to float on the road.

In the mystical schools of Islam, conscious breath is viewed as a primary agency that can support our passage from the alienation of separation toward our merged union with God. The most well known of the Sufi breathing prayers, the *zikr* of the Naqshbandi order, combines a focused remembrance of Allah with strong rhythmic breathing. The Sufis tell us that union with Allah depends on constantly remembering, focusing, and refocusing the mind on the source dimension of all creation, and the powerful breathing of the zikr can transform the dervish seeker so that the consciousness of union descends into his or her body and soul. Jalaluddin Rumi, the great thirteenth-century Sufi mystic and poet, in a declaration about the role that breath plays in religion, our reunification with God, and in our personal healing as well, tells and exhorts us:*

> *bringing breath to life*
> *is the essence of every religion*
> *and the cure for every illness*
>
> *let every breath you take*
> *cleanse the soul of its grief and pain*
> *so it can continue to burn brightly inside you*

After the resurrection it's reported that Jesus blew onto the reassembled disciples to verify the reality of his continued

---

*This and other Rumi quotes are from Will Johnson, *Rumi's Four Essential Practices: Ecstatic Body, Awakened Soul* (Rochester, VT: Inner Traditions, 2010).

existence. What all these reports have in common is that breath can transform the invisibility of God into a feeling presence in your body.

> *the wind is invisible*
> *yet you can feel it*
>
> *god's presence is invisible*
> *but still you can feel it*

Even more germane to the practice I've come to the monastery to explore is the Christian notion of *in spiritu,* the welcoming in of the Holy Spirit into our mind and body, and in spiritu may be easily thought of as inspiration, which is another word we use for inhalation. When we inhale, when we inspire, we welcome the spirit of God into our body where we can feel it as presence. The term *in spiritu* implies that God's presence—the Holy Spirit, the intermediator between God and man—can be transmitted to humans through the inhalation of breath.

> *breath is the agency*
> *through which god makes its presence felt*
> *in your life and body*
> *when you breathe consciously*
> *taking breath deeply into your body*
> *like a holy sacrament*
> *you become one with god*
> *even if just for a little minute*

to breathe god
to take god's spirit into your body
with every inhalation you take
with every inspiration you make
is to become fully human
to join your small self
to the everything of god

More than anything I want to feel inspired in my life. I want not just to breathe but to feel breathed. I want to open to the fullness of God's breath, God's inspiration, and become one with that fullness. I want to directly experience that fullness as felt sensation, felt presence, in my body and mind. It doesn't work for me any longer just to believe in that presence, just to have faith in its existence. I need to feel it. To know it as real. Directly. I want to surrender my body to the breath of God, and so I keep patiently bringing my attention back to my breath as I breathe in . . . as I breathe out . . . as I breathe in once again. Breath is spirit. Let me breathe spirit in.

Entering the Silence
Breathing in Spirit, Breathing out Peace

in the center of your body
underneath the turbulent layer of
    thought
that clouds your mind
and disturbs your peace
is a place of perfect silence

so peaceful
like the depths of an ocean
underneath the stormy waves
undisturbed by what's happening
at the surface of its waters

this place of silent peace
is where god's presence can be felt

this place of silent peace
is home to the holy spirit
like a bird on a branch
the holy spirit
alights on this place of peace
in the center of your body

spirit is fed and nurtured by breath
the more you can breathe
consistently and consciously
into this place in the center of your center
the more you can feel god
directly touching you
caressing you
speaking to you

as you keep remembering
to be aware of your breath
breathing in
breathing out

also remember
to take in the presence of god
the source of all life
on every inhalation
every inspiration

also remember
on every exhalation
every expiration
to let go of the individuality of your life
to become a vessel
that breathes spirit back into god
and radiates peace

nourish yourself
by breathing into the silence
heal yourself
by breathing out peace
to your loved ones
your friends and community
all humans
the planet that we share
the universe we live in
breathing in silence
breathing out peace

become a receiver
of god's silent presence
a transmitter of god's peace

> *breathing god in on the inhalation*
> *spreading peace to all four corners of the*
> *earth and beyond*
> *on the exhalation*

Moderation as the one constant flavor in my life (like an obsession with vanilla or chocolate that keeps you from sampling the other twenty-nine flavors) is suddenly looking overrated. Paul Reps, the American Zen teacher, most closely hit the mark when he said that the way to live a good life is to do everything in moderation, including moderation. Immoderation, when it comes to the awareness of breath, at times floats and lifts me up, and when my inspiration and expiration, my merging with the breath, is so complete it can feel like a kind of ecstasy, like coming back home to myself where I can feel the presence of spirit, God's way of saying, *Hello, I'm here.* Most of the time I might think of immoderation as a bad thing certain to lead me down a path I don't want to take in my life, and for many of us that may be true. But the single-minded focus on the breath that enters and leaves my body, obsessive as it may be, feels like a virtuous immoderation, not at all a vicious one. Breath, after all, is such an automatic event. Focusing on it so single-mindedly feels as though it has nothing at all to do with moderation (why obsessively focus on something that happens anyway whether you're focusing on it or not?). But as challenging as all this is, as dramatic a shift as it is from how I normally go about my life, I'm finding that I quite love doing this, just staying focused as best I can on the

breath, immoderate as it may be. And so I keep breathing in
. . . breathing out . . . breathing . . .

i'm obsessed with my breath
i never want to let it go

some of us
for better or worse
or actually for neither
it's just who we are
feel an irresistible pull
a current
it's a physical force
drawing us in the direction
of what we may use
the word god to describe

and some of us feel
an equally irresistible urgency
to surrender to the breath
doing our best to never let it go
doing our best to forgive ourselves
when we do

Nighttime comes. It feels good to lie down and rest. So
silent. So still. How can I feel so tired from doing so little? The
most effortful action of my day has not been in paying such
close attention to my breath but in constantly remembering to
turn my attention back to it. A lassitude as I lie on my bed. A

strangely exhilarated fatigue . . . I'm not sure what it is. Heavy and floating both. It feels good, already softer, fewer rough edges than when I first arrived. Breathing into the silence, breathing out peace, breathing into the silence, breathing out peace, breathing . . . maybe I can just do this, maybe it is possible just to remember to breathe . . . not feeling quite so daunted as I was yesterday morning when I first woke and tried to remember to remember to remember . . . to remember . . . my breath . . . breathing, breathing, breathing . . . until I lose myself to the night and even breath disappears.

In God's Image

The consciousness that passes as normal in our contemporary world is a consciousness lost in thought. We're too busy thinking to feel, and when we're lost in thought, we effectively lose touch with the feeling presence of the body. So successful is the thinking mind in hijacking our attention and turning us away from feeling much of anything—let alone feeling merged with the everything that is God—that we lose touch with the possibility of God's existence. Clearly, it struck me this morning—as I kept breathing in, kept breathing out—a transition needs to be made to move our attention from the mind that thinks into the body that feels.

Separation from God occurs when you're not welcoming the felt spirit of God directly into your body, and staying lost in thought is the most effective strategy you have for making sure that spirit can't enter. Lost in thought, you can think about God. You can believe in God. You can have faith in God, but you can't experience God as an actual, palpable, felt presence. God's presence can only be directly experienced as a feeling in your body, never as a thought in your mind. We become aware of God knocking on our door through the felt awareness of what Christianity calls the Holy Spirit, which first reveals itself through the flutter of felt sensations that start waking up in the body. On every part of your body, down to the smallest cell, minute little pinprick blips of sensation can be felt to exist, but when you're lost in thought, these sensations go dark and numb. And so it could also be said that when you're lost in thought, your awareness of God goes dark and numb as well.

God is the life that lives you and can be felt as a current that courses through your body. But if you've lost touch with the vibrant streams and flows of sensations in your body, its felt presence usurped by a parade of thoughts that never ends, you're holding back on the current of the life force that wants to flow and express itself through you. The reawakening, then, of a feeling presence—the gradual reemergence of humming, vibratory, tingling sensation all through your body and the felt sense of spaciousness that these sensations reveal—is the first sign that the spirit of God is trying to enter into you.

So what can you do? You can remember to feel and breathe. You can turn your attention away from your thoughts and toward your body, and you can bring the unconscious action of breath back to front and center awareness. Breathing consciously—staying as aware as possible of every relaxed breath you take—is one of the most potent, and altogether natural, tools you have at your disposal to bring the sleeping body back to felt vibrant life. It's as though breath is the nutriment of sensations. Feed the body with deep, full, and conscious breath, and sensations come alive like stars that emerge into the early night sky. Deprive the body of a conscious, relaxed breath, and sensations wither like plants that haven't been watered.

> *to merge with god*
> *is to merge with everything*
> *but instead we feel isolated*
> *alone in the world*
> *separated*
> *even from our own body*
> *whose sensations*
> *we forget to feel*
>
> *for most of us*
> *most of the time*
> *so tied up in thought as we are*
> *the totality of our world*
> *consists of the few cubic inches inside*
>   *our cranium*
>
> *but god includes everything*
>
> *to become one with god*
> *is to expand into the felt wholeness*
> *the holiness*
>
> *to feel whole in yourself*
> *is to feel the whole of your body*

as a unified field
of tactile presence

to stay estranged from god
is to stay trapped inside
the claustrophobic confines of your head

if the felt body is the doorway
to the vastness of god
the discrepancy of scale
between living in your head or in your
*   body*
is immense

i stay lost in thought
and i stay isolated
separate from everything

i bring the feeling presence of my body
*   alive*
and god enters me

In most religious traditions, God is conceived as a transcendental force, at once the original spark that brought the universe into creation and the shepherd who watches over the world and every being in it with compassion and love. The human body, on the other hand, even though the direct object of God's creation, is viewed as in eternal struggle between the gravitational pull of God's love and light and a dark force that causes it to spin off into behaviors that cause us and others pain and suffering. In most traditions the body is looked on as an opportunity to experience God's grace, but also all too often as an obstacle to the witnessing of God's love and to the direct participation in that love.

The body is where we love and experience happiness and kindness toward others, but it's also where anger and hatred live, and our technological prowess keeps creating ever more horrible weapons with which we can hurt, maim, and kill in a second everyone and everything we project our hatred out onto. Sex between loving humans is our most sacred act, and yet the body is also where we experience the tsunamis of lustful desire. When these waves become so large and powerful, they crash upon our beaches of respect toward others and cause us—mostly men against women—to use others to satisfy our unsatisfiable lust and craving with no regard for mutuality. Is it any wonder that rape of innocent women and children becomes a preferred strategy of armies filled with hatred toward those they perceive as their enemy? The body is where sadnesses and fear run rampant, where cravings and aversions play themselves out free of checks and balances.

And yet we're also told that we're created in God's image, that we're reflections in miniature of the gifts and proclivities of God. How is it possible to square this most hopeful of understandings with the ravages that the body is also so capable of executing?

The simplest answer that occurs to me this morning—and I in no way want this to sound simplistic—is that when we're swept away and caught up in raging currents of anger, lust, fear, and sadness; when we're overwhelmed by the potency of their energies like dry brush into which a lighted match has just been dropped, we're completely unaware of the breath. We lose consciousness of our inhalation and our exhalation, of our inspiration and expiration. We lose touch with God. Losing awareness of the breath, we're set adrift from our mooring and heritage as a child of God, like a boat adrift on the ocean with no steerage, no sail, no powering motor; just adrift, getting tossed here and there by energies too powerful to navigate. Lost in thought, we unwittingly imprison our breath inside restrictive walls and muscular tensions of anger, fear, and craving. But when we regain our composure and become again more grounded in our awareness of breath's passage, one breath flowing naturally again into the next, and the next, God starts showing back up. When you breathe and are breathed by God, it's simply not possible to behave in ways that cause pain and suffering to yourself or anyone else.

> *it's said that god giveth life*
> *and god taketh away life*
>
> *it could just as easily be said*
> *that breath giveth life*
> *and breath taketh away life*
>
> *our first inhalation*

> *marks the moment of our birth*
> *our final exhalation*
> *signals our passage into death*

When we hear that we're made in the image of God, it's all too easy to envision God as a larger version of ourselves, and so we anthropomorphize our notion of God as a wise old man or woman sitting on a heavenly throne. But we have this exactly backward. It's we who are made in God's image, not God who is made in ours. According to the Old Testament, God entered into humans and gave them life through a mixture of two things: the dust of Earth and the power of the breath. So to reconnect with the original human that you are, created in the reflected image of God, you want to bring breath back to life so it can be felt blowing into the minute cells of the body, awakening their felt presence.

> *sensation and breath am i*
> *nothing but sensation and breath*

But we don't experience ourselves as sensation and breath. We don't let ourselves feel the shimmering glow of the body, and we hold back on the force of the breath that wants to breathe through us at this moment. And the one is the direct reflection of the other. Instead of sensation and breath, we take up residence in a mind that thinks and a body that scarcely breathes. Separated from sensation and breath, mind concocts a picture, a facsimile, a self-image of who and what you think you are, and the self-image you carry with you is like a concealing mask that covers over your true God-reflecting self. We tend to impose this covering over the front of the body for everyone to see, and this imposition of self-image turns us into imposters. You can feel the self-image out in the front of your body just as you would feel a mask that you fix to your face at a carnival or costume party.

To experience God as an actual, palpable, felt presence, we need to get back in touch with the sensations and breath that self-image conceals. We want to soften and dissolve the mask of self-image—our prides, our ambitions, our wants, our fears—and trust in the feeling presence of the body. Just sensation. Just breath.

> *deeper than the image i hold of myself*
> *is the sensation and breath that i am*
> *my image of myself*
> *is but a pale shadow*
> *of the felt vibrancy that is my birthright*

Underneath the mask, on every part of the body down to the smallest cell, is an oceanic web of minute pinprick blips of sensation, constantly moving and changing, the cellular motes of matter into which life has been blown.

But mostly we have little to no awareness of this great oceanic web of feeling presence. We're lost in the unbidden, random thoughts of our mind that cover over that web like a blanket over a statue that's yet to be unveiled. To resurrect God's presence in our own bodies, we want to bring our *sensational* presence back to life, and just as God did in the moment of Adam's creation, we want to breathe into every little cell of the body, every nook and cranny. God did not just blow life into some of the dust motes that coalesced to form Adam's body. God blew into all of them. Breathing into the entire body in this way brings the tingling, vibratory, humming, buzzing sensations of each and every cell of the body back to felt life.

> *no*
> *you can't take the oxygen in the air*
> *and breathe it into*
> *every cell of the body*
>
> *but yes*
> *you can breathe right into*
> *the body's global feeling presence*
> *stimulating sensation everywhere*
> *breath and sensation meeting*

The practice of Breathing God, of feeling the presence of God as the fundamental ground of your bodily life, is twofold. First, you can shift your awareness away from the thoughts in your mind back to the sensations that exist in every part of the body but which you can't feel when you're lost in the thoughts that feed your self-image.

> *my thoughts are always concerned*
> *with my place in the material world*

but my sensations are the holy spirit's
  way of saying
come
follow me
i'll take you to god

Just by remembering to feel—perhaps passing your awareness at first through each and every part of the body, slowly, methodically, over and over again, to reinforce this remembrance—you can start breaking free from the gravitational pull of the mind that thinks thoughts. The good news gospel is that, through no heroic efforts and expenditures of energy but simply by redirecting and paying attention, sensations start coming back to felt life. Over time, every part of the body can wake up—first one part, then another. And suddenly the ground is prepared for the great leap in which you start to feel the body not as an assortment of individual parts—a hand here, a knee there—but all at once, as a unified field of felt presence.

And then, secondly, you can start relaxing so deeply that the breath you've worked so hard to become conscious of, your inspiration-inhalation, can be felt to stimulate and touch into every single cell of your body. And just as unconscious, restricted breath and a generalized numbness of body are reflections of each other, so too are an awakened body and a more freely flowing breath. In truth, the twofold practice—bringing the feeling presence and breath both to life—can't really be divided into two, as the one reinforces the other. If you bring body to life, breath naturally becomes fuller. Through becoming more aware of the breath, and surrendering to its potency, sensations come alive. Breathing into the whole body, then, is a direct reflection of that original breath in which God gave life to Adam by blowing into all the dust motes of his as-yet lifeless body.

And here I feel a real dilemma because my mind and my body are telling me two opposite things, championing two perspectives that couldn't be more different from each other. And what's more, each sounds completely true.

My mind objects strongly to the notion that every breath I take could be felt to touch every facet of my entire body because I know as scientific fact and certainty that I don't breathe into every cell of my body, only into my lungs. And yet today there've been moments when I could feel each inhalation touching into and awakening sensation everywhere in my body, stimulating the latent shimmer of every single cell all at once.

> *two breaths*
> *one bringing oxygen*
> *to my lungs*
> *the other stimulating*
> *felt presence*
> *throughout my body*

Today, there've been moments in which breath, in addition to being the source of oxygen that my body so needs as its most vital food, has also become a force that could be felt touching my body, not just into my lungs alone, but everywhere. How can this be? From the perspective of my mind, what I've just said sounds ridiculous, but from the perspective of those moments of awakened body and breath, I can see how both are equally true. One breath keeps me alive. The other breath awakens God in me.

> *the scientific explanation*
> *for why we breathe*
> *is one of those rare instances*
> *where knowledge ends up*
> *disempowering us*

Because we're so certain in our physiological knowledge that the air we inhale goes into our lungs and no farther, we don't let ourselves consider that there could be another quality of breath that could be felt to stimulate sensation in every single cell of the body. And it's precisely this latter quality of breath—which can be felt to illuminate the entire body on the inhalation—that allows God's presence to be felt entering us.

But still, how can we make this happen? Centered in the perspective of thought, I know that, when I breathe in, oxygen in the air enters my lungs. But when thought evaporates and I once again am able to relax and settle into a global awareness of the feeling presence of my entire body, a whole different quality of breath can be felt occurring in which breath and body, not just breath and lungs, strangely start to commingle.

As I breathe in, I breathe into the felt awareness of the entire body, nothing left out, every part of me included as an integral component of God's creation.

To breathe in this way, I have to relax deeply. When I examine my body while I'm lost in thought, I become aware of places in my body, especially in my cranium, that have tensed because the tension has become a necessary component of the action of thought. When I relax the tension throughout the entire body, and when thought evaporates, even if only temporarily, I shift perspective into what almost feels like another world in which I can feel the whole of the body as a unified field of felt sensation. And a body that is so whole in feeling presence is a body in which breath can be felt stimulating sensation into every one of its cells on every inhalation.

A fundamental law of physics is that something can exist only as a wave or a particle of matter. It's either one or the other and can never be both. But then there are experiments that demonstrate that light is a wave, but others that equally convincingly prove that it's a particle. In a world of paradox, breath can apparently affect me in two seemingly contradictory ways.

> *breath is not just a thing to*
> *   observe*
> *but a force to surrender to*
> *just as god's presence is not just*
> *   something to believe in*
> *but a force to surrender to*

Breathing God

step one
at first
become passively aware
that you're breathing
breath going in
breath going out
over and over and over again

step two
as you're able to extend the length of
     time
that you stay lodged in your breath
rather than adrift in your mind
you start imagining
spirit entering into you
with every inspired inhalation you take
peace radiating out from you
through every expiring exhalation you
     make

step three
and now you go beyond
observation and imagination both
you move into direct experience

as you keep observing breath
as you keep imagining
spirit entering you on the inhalation

peace radiating from you on the
     exhalation
you're inevitably drawn back down
into your body
right into the feeling presence
in the totality of your body
and you're ready finally
to take the final step
and surrender to the potency
that is the breath
to surrender to the feeling of god
being breathed into every cell of your
     body
with every inspired inhalation you take

with every inhalation you take
don't just breathe into your lungs
or your chest
or any isolated place in your body
instead breathe into the feeling presence
of your entire body
and do this
through an inspired gesture of letting go
to the potency of your inhalation

breathing god
into your whole body
on every inhalation you take
recreates the original breath

through which god breathed life into
    adam

in every surrendered inspiration you take
you're born again
just as you were born
in your first inspiration
on which you entered this world

with every expiration you give
you rehearse
the last expiration
you'll ever make
you let go of yourself completely
and enter back into god's embrace

breathing god into life
expiring into god
god breathing god
let every cell of your body
every atom of every cell
every subatomic particle of every
    atom
be consumed by the breath

it's said that god is a wind
that moves across the water
welcome god as the surrendered
    inspiration of breath

that moves through and across your
    physical body
composed as it is of some 70 percent
    water

how can you
more palpably feel
the inspiration of breath
as the holy spirit
entering into every felt cell of your body
on every breath you take

----◄ ►----

The practice of Breathing God is a practice of surrendering to the breath, submitting yourself to its potency, surrendering to the presence and force of God that exists in each and every breath you take. Surrendering to the breath in this way, I come up against everything that resists it. I come up against walls of soft tissue that has hardened and won't let my chest expand on the inspiration and contract on the expiration. Walls of anger. Walls of sadness and fear. Walls of pride. Walls of craving for things I don't have and walls of antipathy toward things I do.

But surrendering to the breath smokes these resistances out of their hiding places where they can't be seen or felt. Breathing in this way helps me get in touch with the holdings and resistances I'm unconsciously enacting that keep the direct experience of God remote and unavailable. And so, as challenging as it may be, I let the resistances emerge. I let the holdings come up where they can be felt. And because they can be felt, I can now start letting them go, releasing the tensions. And as the underlying tensions that so create and support my estrangement from God start relaxing and releasing, breath becomes fuller and the feeling presence of God comes closer. Ultimately, Breathing God is a healing practice, healing me of everything I hold onto that keeps God away.

I know that I couldn't have come close to glimpsing the potent possibility of every breath touching into and stimulating sensation in every cell of my body on the first day I arrived. I had to spend time observing first, bringing the automatic process of breath to awareness, watching breath go in and out, in and out, over and over again, and patiently bringing my awareness back to the breath whenever I realized I'd lost that awareness by going off again into endless trains of thought.

And the next step, imagining God riding on the inhalation as it enters my body while the peace of God radiates out of my body on the exhalation, helps prepare me even further by forcing me to become even more aware of how the whole of the body, not just the lungs, is involved in the action of breath.

Today, breath took a giant leap and revealed a whole new octave of influence and affect. Today, at least for a few moments, I felt how breath could touch into my entire body. And as breath and felt body merged into a single coterminous phenomenon, I started to feel God entering me, entering me on every inhalation, the force of breath as the presence of God that, in a time long ago, first transformed the dust of the original human into a living being, created from God and in his image.

Day Four

From My Head to My Belly

relaxing into a breath
that can be felt through my whole body
takes me on a journey
from my head
to my belly
from the crowded city of thoughts
to the spacious land of presence

The gravitational center of modern men and women has risen precariously upward from its natural foundation in the belly into the more ethereal regions of the head, and while this has been an intellectual ascent, it's not been a spiritual one. Asked where you feel you exist in your body, far more people will reply, "Why, up in my head, of course, where my thoughts reside" than, "Down here in my belly, where my presence can be felt." We've become top heavy, unstable. We've lost our ballast and moorings—we've lost our breath—and find ourselves floating, aloft and adrift, up in the airy realm of thought, like a hot-air balloon that's lost its ability to come back down to

Earth. We take for truth the pronouncements and perspectives of our personal thoughts, even though contradictory positions can almost always be supported and rationalized as equally real and true. Someone who's spouting nonsense that he nevertheless believes to be truth is sometimes characterized as *full of hot air*. Caught up in the ricocheting thoughts in our head, we've lost touch with the calm, stable ground of felt presence. Out of touch with the feeling presence in our belly, we can't find our way back to God.

"Don't believe everything your mind tells you" has become a popular New Age bumper-sticker slogan with more truth to it than many of the questionable notions and beliefs our mind keeps spewing as though they were irrefutable truth itself. Like the exponential multiplication of brooms that bedevil the sorcerer's apprentice from the old Disney cartoon, thought begets more thought and then even more until—much like the apprentice—we're left overwhelmed, exhausted, and unable to deal with the mess we've made. Thought has won out over feeling presence and become the god we worship, so we identify ourselves with the speaker of our internal, involuntary monologue, who rambles on constantly inside our head, and turn away from the feeling radiating out from our belly.

> *my prayer for today*
>
> *help me drop down*
> *out of the meandering thoughts in*
>   *my head*
> *into the felt presence in my belly*

There are two primary strategies I draw on that help me drop down. First, I can simply shift my focus, gently; let go of the power that thought has had over me for so long; and engage in what might almost be considered a radical act: I turn my attention from my head to my belly. Once I'm there, I just give myself permission to feel . . . whatever's there . . . just feeling what the presence in my belly actually feels like. There are no thoughts in my belly. My belly speaks to me in the silent language of felt sensations. Out from my belly I sense a radiating force field, a strange admixture of felt shimmer and space. As soon as I start feeling this presence in my belly, thoughts begin diminishing.

The trick is to enact this shift in focus without disturbing feeling presence artificially. You don't have to manufacture feeling presence. It's always here, waiting for you simply to feel it. Nor do you have to try to shut thoughts down. Just shift into feeling presence, and thoughts start shutting down on their own. The mechanism that reinforces them shuts off, and thought just fades away like the voice of the computer in the film *2001: A Space Odyssey,* which, after its energy source is cut off, just starts slowing down . . . fading . . . fading . . . until it goes silent.

And second, dropping down from my head to my belly entails a simple acknowledgment of our place in the universe as Earthlings, bound forever to our mother Earth through the umbilical cord of gravity. I can far more easily drop from my head to my belly if I can give up my bracing against the ubiquitous force of gravity and give in to its pull instead. Ordinarily, I brace myself against the force of Earth's gravity to keep from toppling over, but this bracing brings tension into my body and a stiffening in my neck, which in turn keeps me locked in the thoughts in my head. If I can let go of bracing against gravity . . .

> *and bracing is bracing*
> *if you're bracing against gravity*
> *aren't you also bracing*
> *against the presence of god*

. . . if I can surrender the weight of my body to the ubiquitous pull of gravity without toppling over, this dropping down out of the head into the belly occurs spontaneously, like holding a stone in your hand, dropping the stone, and watching the stone plummet. What this requires is a simple gesture of relaxation and letting go—relaxing tensions in the body that cause pain, letting go of tensions in the cranium that spur thoughts—which allows you to drop down but still stand upright, tall, in grace, not bracing anywhere against gravity but not toppling over either.

I wake this morning and remember a dream from last night that's almost embarrassingly obvious. I'm in a department store. I've been shopping on the top floor for attractive electrical appliances that I don't really need, but it's great fun to check out the latest and greatest contraptions. Finally, it's time to let the fascination go, and I move down through a convoluted maze of escalators to the ground floor where undergarments are on sale.

Dropping down, dropping down, dropping down. Very curiously . . . when I drop down in this way and my center of gravity becomes more rooted in my belly . . . something inside me can be felt to rise up:

> *rooted in my belly*
> *i'm drawn upward*
> *uplifted*
> *like a flower*
> *awakening to the morning light*
> *my heart radiates*

Almost as a response to this humbling gesture of dropping down—like some kind of spiritual manifestation of Isaac Newton's second law of motion, which tells us that, for every action, there's an equal and opposite reaction—I feel inner energies rising, floating up, weightlessly, like the sensation that happens when you've carried a friend on your shoulders and then set him back down. It's as though a force analogous to Earth's energy but acting in an opposite direction of pull is drawing me upward. Earth draws me down to itself, which then allows this awakened energy to uplift me, but when I rise up in this way, I don't go back to the place where my mind keeps thinking thoughts. I go to a place where my heart keeps radiating love.

> *i drop my head*
> *at the onset of inhalation*
> *my chin falls forward*
> *air rushes in effortlessly*

as i drop down
air fills my body
i land upon the surface
of a spiritual trampoline

something inside me
bounces back up

grounded in the feeling presence
of my stable belly
breath breathes me
my heart opens
my whole body awakens

It's when I drop down in this way that I'm able to locate the secret passage in the center of my body. It feels as much like space as sensation. It comes into the felt equivalent of view, and it feels as though it's beckoning me.

listen to me
by feeling me

so says spirit

come this way
deeper
into the middle of your torso
from where you can feel
your whole body all at once

enter through this sacred opening
and walk on in

I don't know where this secret passage leads to. I don't know what's there. It's mysterious. I should probably be wary, but I'm not. Because the secret passage is . . . inviting. There's something about it, the quality of its space, its sensation, radiating out from the center of my torso, that just feels . . . right—even though I can't explain why. I trust it. I feel like a compilation of tiny bits of iron drawn to its magnetic pull. So here goes nothing. Just keep breathing and surrendering to a force that feels as though it's magnetically drawing me to it.

I'm remembering a phrase from the Old Testament that always struck me as peculiar, and it's stimulating a whole new level of understanding about the breath. When God would get angry at his children, the Israelites, he'd utter the worst imprecation possible. He would call them a stiff-necked people. He didn't call them out for being ill mannered, ungrateful, disrespectful. The God of the Old Testament called out his children for having stiff necks. What?!

What possibly might a stiff neck in an Old Testament context signify? Resistance, stubbornness, perhaps, digging in one's heels. Love of individual self over respect toward elders and community. Just the kinds of things authoritarian dads don't like to see in their kids. But to the extent that we become lost in thought and turn our back on the presence of

God, we all become stiff-necked people. Chronic stiffness in the slender connection between your head and the rest of your body creates a barrier to the flow of the life force, which wants to pass freely through you, from head to toe and back again. Chronic stiffness in your neck ensures that the gravitational center of your self stays where it is, high in your head, where you remain lost in thought. Chronic stiffness in your neck doesn't let the you in your head drop down and away into the feeling presence in your torso.

A stiff neck doesn't move. It stays still, its flexibility gradually lost. Trading off the natural resilience it was born with for the artificial stiffness it's created, it keeps me lost in elevated thought. So my insight this afternoon is:

> *to soften the stiffness*
> *let my neck*
> *stay moving*
> *while I'm breathing*

The joints between the vertebrae in my neck are no different from joints anywhere in my body. They're designed for one purpose and one purpose only, and that's to move. If I don't let them move, I'm resisting God's design. If I can relax the frozen stiffness in my neck, the force of breath can be felt to move through it, not unlike how a wave moves through a body of water. I don't have to do anything to make this motion happen. I just have to relax, soften, let go, and the natural force of the breath will keep my neck moving and my head bobbing. When my neck moves naturally, subtly, in coordination with my breath, the entire spine starts to release, and the tension that keeps me locked in thoughts begins to slacken and unclench.

Watch what happens when you're walking down the street and you become lost in a thought. Haven't you become one of the stiff-necked people again?

Releasing the Neck

sitting in a chair
or cross-legged on the floor
at the onset of inhalation
relax the tension
in your neck
the holding quality
that keeps your neck
stiff
still
unmoving

at the onset of inhalation
let go

your chin drops toward your chest
your neck rounds backward
as air rushes in
through this unobstructed
    channel
your head glides backward
and floats up

when you exhale
your head floats back down
breathing in
breathing out
your neck constantly moving
your head constantly circling

when there's motion in your neck
when your head constantly floats
thoughts have no ground
to stand on

The practice of Releasing the Neck can be entered into at any time whether you're formally praying or meditating or simply going about your life. The following Breathing Prayer is a more exaggerated version of Releasing the Neck, and you can explore it for short periods of time. It helps release residual stiffness in the neck and soften chronic tension throughout the entire spine.

Breathing Prayer
Awakening the Spine, Opening the Heart

sitting or kneeling on the ground
perhaps on a soft pillow
to cushion your legs

start by exhaling completely
and collapsing forward
dropping your head
down toward your chest

slumping down farther
the lower torso rounding backward
as your upper body collapses down
your head bowed
your hands resting on your thighs
a gesture of submission

wait

on the inhalation
your body starts uncoiling
rising back up
like a snake
enchanted by a charmer's flute
your spine lengthening
upward
the lower back comes forward
the upper body straightens
the arms reach out to the sides
reaching
reaching
the head looks up
the front of your body opens
a gesture of exultation and joy

at the onset of exhalation
as your body starts compressing down
bring your arms back down
into your lap

to complete your gesture of prayer

the movement plays back and forth
between the poles
of exultation and submission
let each inspired inhalation
fill you up completely
let each expired exhalation
empty you out completely

do this breathing prayer
for five or ten minutes
or as long as you like
as often as you like

———◄►———

Day passes into night. Every day my awareness of breath becomes a bit more stable, but still it comes and goes. When I lose awareness of breath, my internal elevator shoots me up into my head where my thoughts are on full display. But when I remember to remember my breath, the elevator goes back down, down, farther down, and lets me off in my abdomen. The elevator rises through bracing and tension, goes down through a gesture of relaxation and letting go. It feels like my belly's calling out to me, calling me down, summoning me to let go, to release my obsession with thought, reminding me that the best bargains are always to be found in the basement. As I drift away into a light sleep, I keep breathing and relaxing, breathing and letting go, breathing and free falling, down . . . down.

God Is What Happens When I Disappear

I wake up to a strange mix of exhaustion, elation, awe. I should put *wake up* in quotation marks because I don't feel I actually got much sleep to wake up from. All day yesterday my breath had mostly been slow and placid as I kept focusing on dropping down into my belly, both at the onset of inhalation and through a long and extended exhale. But as I went to bed last night, the cycles of my breath suddenly sped up on their own. It was as though I'd been taking a pleasant daytime walk on a path along a canal when, just before going to bed, I slipped and fell into the water, into a channel whose current was strong, and my breath stayed there most of the night, unable to free itself from the current, like a needle on a vinyl record, stuck in a groove, the sounds repeating over and over and over. There was no way I could break free, not that I really wanted to. In and out . . . in and out . . . breath breathing itself, breath driving itself, and I kept waiting for it to wind down and fade away, so I could do the same. And it never felt like that really happened. Like a song that you can't get out of your head, breath wouldn't let me be. I wasn't so much breathing as being breathed, all through my felt body, breath after breath, all night long, and it caused my body to buzz. I couldn't resist the breath or the buzzing. I had to let go. But what was I letting go of, and what into?

> *focusing your entire attention*
> *on the breath*
> *stirs and awakens felt sensations*
> *throughout the body*
>
> *once sensations are awakened*
> *you just let go*
> *into the vortex*
> *in the center of your felt body*
> *that keeps drawing you to itself*
>
> *riding on the breath*
> *you keep moving*
> *moving*
> *swept along on a current*
> *that takes you to a place*
> *where the i has far less sovereignty*
>
> *when i drop*
> *from my head to my belly*
> *thoughts in my head*
> *start falling away*

and when thought disappears
what happens
to the person
who's thinking those thoughts

We all have the same word for the person who thinks thoughts. We call that person "I." But when I drop down into my belly, not only do thoughts disappear, but the speaker of those thoughts disappears right along with them. When there's no thought, there's no I. And when the I in me disappears . . . God is there.

The ego, this dominating sense of I, separate from everything that exists outside myself, is fortified and sustained by bringing tension into the body. For the ego to reign supreme, feeling presence needs to be stifled, dialed down, and breath needs to be held back, restrained. As I write this, it strikes me that my words may sound like a condemnation of the ego. That's not my intention, so it feels important to acknowledge that there's nothing at all wrong with egoic consciousness. We need to get good at it and use it skillfully and well as we navigate our way through the world into which we've been born. The problem with the holding pattern of the ego is that it would like us to believe that it's the only possible setting on the lens of consciousness. It's not. As extraordinary as are its skills, the ego still depends for its nurturance on resistance to a feeling energy and a breath that, when relaxed into, reveal a very different perspective and understanding about the life we've been born into.

When we're able to soften and let go of the egoic fixation, it's not just a softening of bodily tension that occurs.

Consciousness, too, shifts, and the claustrophobia of what we call ego is replaced by the expansive breadth and breath of what we call God. Why would I choose tension and resistance to a life of relaxation and letting go?

> *when the i in me is large*
> *the god in me is small*
> *when the i in me is small*
> *the god in me is large*
>
> *it's the i in me*
> *that blocks the god in me*
>
> *to let go*
> *to make room for god*
> *i have to relax*
> *and let tension go*
>
> *when i let tension go*
> *i goes as well*
> *i disappears*
> *and suddenly*
> *the vibrancy of god*
> *is there*

Moses is reported to have asked God, "Where shall I find you?" and God responded, "Abandon your ego [what Islam refers to

as *nafs*], and then you shall find me." The Sufis tell us much the
same thing when they cryptically say, "You need to die before
you die." They're not in any way suggesting a premature death
of the physical body. What they want to see die is the unques-
tioned belief in the egoic perspective. They want you to soften
the holding patterns of tension that create the egoic fixation, for
the exclusivity of this perspective creates a barrier, a concealing
veneer that covers over the felt awareness of God. As you melt
these barriers, your I melts down as well. To die before you die
means to come alive while you are alive, to be born anew into
the breath of life and the vitality of the body.

Christians tell us to let go of our egoic agendas and trust
in God's instead: "Not my will but thy will." And Shloma
Majeski, a contemporary Hasidic rabbi, writes: "*Simchah*, joy,
also involves letting go, but it is a very different type of letting
go. One does not lose control one transfers control. When a
person experiences true joy, he lets go of himself, but he con-
nects to something higher, G-d. He lets go of his petty ego
and makes it possible for a dimension of his identity that is far
deeper and far truer to surface."*

Much of the process of welcoming God's felt presence back
into my life is one of softening the patterns of tension and
holding I've introduced into my body in an effort to craft

---

*From chapter 10 in Shloma Majeski, *The Chassidic Approach to Joy* (New
York: Sichos in English, 1995).

an image of how I want to be seen. All of us have a different version of who we are in this world: a high-powered business-person, the life of the party, a good parent, a gang member needing to prove his credentials on the street, a poet, a just-the-facts rationalist, a team player, a server of others, a taker from others, and on and on. The list of personas is endless. Some of them we may feel we've been born into, but most of them are consciously chosen, and as different as they all are, as we all are, they all share one important feature in common: they all depend on different patterns of muscular holding and tension that you bring into your body—tension that not just incidentally holds back on the force of breath— to create the mask of identity that you want to project out in the world in this moment, like an actor playing a part. All the many different ways you need to bring tension into your body to create the image of how you want to be seen in this moment compromise the vibrancy in the underlying cells of your body or exaggerate their intensity.

> *to receive god's presence*
> *i have to let go of*
> *me*
>
> *i stops the flow of god*
>
> *i is the part of me*
> *that resists being the whole of god*
> *when i starts dissolving*
> *when i starts disappearing*

god steps in to fill the void

the i in me
so dependent
on crafted patterns
of tension in the body
and restrictions to the breath
is like a crafted idol
that the three great monotheistic
   religions
viewed as so very much less than
the one god

And so I'm called upon to let go of my willful resistance to God's presence, to soften my rigid holdings, to dissolve my mask so I can settle back into the reflected image that God's made me in. And apparently all I need to do is just keep surrendering to my breath. Breath by breath, I soften and heal the rigidities within that create the blockages to God's felt presence.

The practice of Breathing God doesn't require any kind of heroic forcible effort to take in the maximum amount of breath on every inhalation. It's far more an act of surrender and letting go, a sudden release and relaxation throughout the entire body at the onset of inhalation. So it's not about forcing anything. It's about letting go. When it comes to Breathing God, the New Age trope *let go and let God* couldn't be more accurate.

let go
and let god

just breathe
eventually your breath
will breathe you

ride upon the current of breath
letting go to it
letting it take you
wherever it wants

free the breath
awaken the body
silence the mind
disappear into god

how much god
am i able to surrender to
on the next inhalation i take

The egoic mind is like a fixed vantage point, a fixed setting on the lens of consciousness, but when I let go and let God, the setting broadens considerably. What was formerly so anchored to a singular held perspective starts coming undone, breaks apart, like Humpty Dumpty after the fall, and is replaced by a phenomenon of felt flow instead. In place of the hardened fixity in the center of my head, a constant stream of feeling presence can be felt to pass through, flowing, constantly changing, never stopping anywhere and hardening back into an egoic fixity. Just as individual droplets of water come together to create a flowing stream, so do minute liberated sensations mass

together into a stream-like flow to replace the frozen fixedness
of my I.

> *aligning myself*
> *with the current of god's river*
> *the life force*
> *that constantly flows through me*
>
> *we don't have to create*
> *the presence of god in us*
> *it's already there*
> *and has always been there*
> *all we have to do*
> *is dissolve the egoic barriers*
> *that keep that presence contained*
> *under wraps*
> *unavailable to us*
> *out of touch*
> *out of breath*

I fall asleep early after dinner. It's still light out; night hasn't
yet come, but my eyes don't want to stay open.

Healing the Separation

I splits the world irrevocably into two by creating an impenetrable wall between *me* and *everything else*. *I* is like a liquid in a bottle. Everything inside the bottle of the body is exclusively me. Everything outside the bottle is other than me, and the consciousness that passes as normal in the world views this separation as incontrovertible fact.

However, a division of the world into what's me and what's not me is not the only possible conclusion we can come to about how reality is constructed. It's more a development of consciousness rather than an intrinsic condition, a man-made construction rather than a God-given one. Although the creation of this wall through our evolved ability to self-identify and think thoughts sets us far apart from the other animals we share this planet with, these skills come with a price. You have to tense your body and hold back the breath in order to function as an autonomous ego, to create what the Sufi mystic Rumi referred to as the *consciousness of separation*. Even though you need the egoic contraction to function in society as an individual body, it still causes pain and tension that

80

doesn't just generate the force field of the wall. It also blocks God's presence.

━━━━●▶━━━━

An exclusivity that forever separates self from other will breed compressed feelings of disconnection, alienation, loneliness. And this exclusivity doesn't just keep feeling states of connection, inclusion, and joining with others remote; it keeps God's palpable presence from entering the body and transforming those feelings. It's as though the egoic mind, for its survival, needs to remain eternally quarantined inside the head, afraid to step outside its domain, afraid to let go and let God. On its inner throne it reigns supreme, but the price we pay for laying claim to this throne, and never leaving it, is that we forfeit our direct participation in God.

━━━━●▶━━━━

All physical objects share two contradictory characteristics. Most obviously, they're all unique conglomerations of matter, they all occupy their own physical space, they're all separate from every other physical object. But, and much less obviously, they're also all connected to an underlying ground state that permeates the entire world of objects and binds every one of them into a single piece. From the perspective of this alternative dimension, objects are not just separate from one another, they're also unified with everything that is. And somehow every object of the universe partakes of both these contradictory characteristics.

Mostly, however, we obsess about the perspective of separation and avoid acknowledging the underlying dimension of unification. And it's not difficult to understand why. You can't see this ground state. It's invisible. You can't measure it or quantify it in any way. The only way to know it is to feel it. And in order to feel it, you have to let go of the hold of the egoic exclusivity. Rumi called the felt awareness of this ground state the *consciousness of union,* for when we dissolve the exclusively egoic perspective of body and mind, we're given a glimpse of an alternative, more embodied consciousness that no longer feels so separate from everything but intimately joined and connected instead.

> *the consciousness of separation*
> *i feel separate from god*
> *the consciousness of union*
> *i feel joined to god*
>
> *bringing breath to awareness*
> *and then surrendering to its potency*
> *is as effective a transforming agent as*
> *   we have*
> *to move consciousness*
> *from separation into union*
>
> *breath is the agent of god*
> *taking you on a journey*
> *from multiplicity*
> *to oneness*

Underlying a world governed by separation and its unsettling feeling of disjunction—that somehow life is passing you by, like a landscape out a train window—is a deep ground state in which you and your body feel intimately merged with everything you ordinarily view as so separate. Instead of a nagging feeling of dissociation, you find your way back down and in, letting go of the obstacles of tension and emotional history that block that descent, back into the center of your center, back to a place deep inside that experiences itself, *feels* itself, even if for only a little moment, as intrinsically bonded to everything that is.

The radical and sudden tapping into this alternative feeling state of union, on the part of a few of our ancestors, must have been the source of the inspiration that created the monotheistic religions.

> *union*
> *is the feeling state*
> *of monotheism*
>
> *just as*
>
> *separation*
> *is the feeling state*
> *of egoic exclusivity*
> *and multiple idols*

The feeling of union is broadly expansive, even as large as the universe itself, while the feeling of separation is contracted, compressed, painfully claustrophobic.

in union
body no longer experiences itself
as separate from anything else

in union
body aligns itself
with the felt stream
of flowing sensations
that permeates everything

in union
body has found a way
to relax its physical tensions
and restricted patterns of breath
and starts feeling merged
with everything it can perceive
to exist outside itself

now reread the poem
and replace the word union
with the word god

And this is why it's so important to make a distinction between the physical matter of the body and the feeling presence of the body. Physical matter can never share physical space with other objects of matter. But the body can become so surrendered to the breath that its felt presence doesn't just come alive. It starts radiating outward, out beyond the surface of the body, far out, until you perceive yourself mingling with everything you can see, no matter how distant—the visual field simultaneously taking up residence in the place inside you that thoughts used to occupy—and the exclusivity of the *you* in you melts away and is replaced by the presence of God.

Lodged in egoic separation, you may banish union into exile, but you can never be wholly successful, as you can never completely expel your deepest self from yourself. The felt dimension of union is always here, always a part of you, hovering around you, tickling you, like the psychic equivalent of an amputated limb that still itches. Even though the egoic mind, for its survival, does its best to banish the unified feeling state from awareness, it can't destroy that state.

———◄►———

But, my mind interjects, I *am* separate from every other physical object in the universe of objects, all of whom are separate from one another as well. True, but this fractured vision of the world as a universe of individual, discreet objects that can never share the same physical space, as accurate as it is to describe the world of visible reality, is conceived in a mind that resists feeling the tactile sensations of the body and holds back the natural force of the breath. Separation defines the structure of physical reality, but experiential reality reveals something additional and altogether different.

Experiential reality has little to do with images and ideas, concepts and theories. It's based not on thought but on feeling presence. It reveals its perspective through awakened sensation and breath. To align myself with the quality of consciousness that enables me to function in the world as an individual separate from everything I perceive to exist outside myself, I unwittingly have to hold back both the river of felt sensations that wants to flow through my physical body and the breath that animates the river's current. When I'm able to resurrect the feeling presence of the body through revitalizing the fullness of breath through the practice of Breathing God, the barrier that separates me from the external world of sights and sounds starts coming down. The force field surrounding my physical body, created through resisting sensations and breath, like an impermeable bubble that keeps me in and everything else out, starts weakening and eventually pops.

Ultimately, both union and separation are real. It's just that they're diametrically different settings on the lens through which we view reality. To function as a whole human being means being able to operate on either setting whenever each— work or prayer—is appropriate: on the one hand able to function as a loving contributing individual in society, on the other able to dissolve oneself into the presence of God.

Breathing Sensation, Vision, and Sound

breathing in
breathing out
body awakens
from head to foot
a stream of felt shimmer
breathing in
breathing out

ordinarily the visual field

looks so out there
out in the greater wide world
and you conceive of yourself
as so in here
inside your body
but this distinction
between inner and outer
is less an inherent reality
than a function
of the fixed setting
of the egoic mind
that depends
for the prolongation
of its existence
on an elaborate pattern of tension
throughout the tissues of the body
which blunts feeling presence
and holds back
the power of the breath

by relaxing the tension
the holding in the body's tissues
the resistance to the body's breath
is resolved
feeling presence expands
reaches out
starts commingling
with the fields of vision and sound
and merges with them

when you relax completely
breath coming in
breath going out
the body coming alive
open your eyes
soften the hardened wall of separation
at the front of your body
and your felt presence
starts bonding with the visual field
the unbreachable barrier
separating you from the visual field
softening and dissolving
as though the visual field
is no longer other than you
but part of you
the visual limb
of your larger body of experience

when you relax completely
breath coming in
breath going out
the body coming alive
open your ears
soften tension
and the sounds you can hear
start entering you
melding with you
no longer other than you
but part of you

the auditory limb
of your larger body of experience

sensation
vision
sound
are all limbs of your body of god
they no longer speak to you
of separation
but blend together
like dye added to water

when sensation
vision
and sound
coalesce in this way
a doorway appears
a crack in the fabric
of the world of appearances
you glide through
and are separate no more
drawn instead
into the unified feeling presence of god

when breath becomes fluid
and free
breathing body back into felt life
you can start breathing
not just into the whole of your physical body

but into your larger body of experience
comprised of sensations felt
vision seen
sound heard

breathing into the awareness of what you feel
breathing into the awareness of what you see
breathing into the awareness of what you hear
one after the other
eventually all at once

feel what you feel
then add what you see
to what you feel
then add what you hear
to what you feel and see

The key to experiencing the merging of your three primary sensory fields—sensations, vision, and sound—is to broaden your awareness so that your focus is no longer on a single part of a field but on the whole of the fields (God is wholeness!): feeling not just a part of the body but the whole of the body, seeing not just an isolated object in the visual field but the whole of the field, hearing not just a single sound but the entirety of the symphony of sounds, and eventually doing all of this at once, like rubbing your tummy while patting your head while hopping up and down on one foot. Sometimes you may just want to rub your tummy. Sometimes you may add the patting of your head. Sometimes you do all three at once.

As I keep breathing, in and out, aware of the phenomenon of breath that I ordinarily take so for granted, the whole of my body eventually starts coming alive, a unified field of shimmering wave-like sensations, from head to foot. Grounded in this unified feeling state, I can then open my eyes. First, I let myself see the whole of the visual field as a unified field rather than focusing on any one object to the exclusion of everything else. And then I invite the visual field to become part of me, not separate from me, to enter into me, not to stay outside. Softening the tension at the front of my body, I start falling into the visual field, dissolving myself into it, while everything I see simultaneously rushes into me, right into my center, strangely commingling, strangely merging.

Then I add sounds. The visual field is ever and always in front of me, sensations occupy the center of my felt world, and sounds enter me through my right and left sides. Sounds are like the horizontal bar that a tightrope walker uses to stabilize herself when she's walking across a slender rope. Adding sounds to my coterminous awareness of the fields of sensation and vision stabilizes my experience of God's unified state even further. Sensations, vision, and sound. I keep on feeling breath enter every single cell of my *physical body*, but my *experiential body* has now expanded beyond my physical body, so this afternoon I experiment with breathing not just into the cells of my physical body but into every little cell of the field of vision as well, every little cell of the field of sounds.

> *god is directly experienced*
> *as the unified field*
> *the invisible substratum of union*

that underlies the world of appearances
the single source of light
out of which all the objects of the world
like holographic images
are projected

to breathe god
is to breathe into the wholeness
of the world of appearances
until i become commingled
with all the sensory fields
and enter into
the feeling state of union

———◄———

Breathing God is a practice of profound *personal* healing. I hesitate to embellish it by labeling it a practice of *spiritual* healing—which implies that it's somehow of a different nature from practices of personal healing—because personal healing demands that we ultimately address our separation from God, our separation from the unified state. Underneath the pain of all of our personal upsets is the pain of this separation, and the practice of Breathing God helps resolve and heal the source of this pain. But the practice could have an even broader application of healing beyond the personal, and I feel overcome with a vision of hope as I write this:

the practice of Breathing God
could heal not just me
but us

If a Jew, a Christian, and a Muslim were to come together for even ten short days and commit to exploring this way of breathing, by the end of their time in one another's company they would all be in so similar a condition of consciousness that any lingering enmity between them would be exposed for how foolish it is. A Jew who successfully takes on the practice of Breathing God will uncover a feeling presence, imbued with love, that is not one iota different from that of the Christian or Muslim who is equally exploring the practice. And this only makes sense, for Judaism, Christianity, and Islam share an identical monotheistic paradigm. There's only one God, each would say, using whatever word or utterance their religion uses for the name of God, so how could the felt consciousness of union for a Jew be any different from the felt consciousness of union that his or her Muslim and Christian brothers and sisters are experiencing?

The monotheistic impulse had to have been based on a sudden awakening to the dimension of felt union. Such a revelation not only exposes a whole new understanding of how reality is constructed, it also heals so much of the personal pain we feel when we resist the potency of union's presence, and why wouldn't the source figures of Christianity, Judaism, and Islam want this for their people? Oneness, not separation (and the multiplicity of gods it gives rise to), is suddenly viewed by the early monotheists as the basis of religious life.

Jews know this in what they refer to as the watchword of their faith: *Hear O Israel, the Lord our God, the Lord is one.* Christianity further analyzes the oneness by pointing out the roles of the son and the Holy Spirit (if the father is the source of God, the ground state, the son is the expression of creation, the world of appearances, and the Holy Spirit is the felt force communicating between them). Islam views *everything* as an expression of Allah. The one God. And the one God can't be different for Judaism, for Christianity, for Islam.

It's time, past time really, that we heal the enmity and separation that exists among the three great monotheistic religions, the mistrust, suspicion, and outright hatred that they sometimes hold toward one another: Christians blaming the Jews for killing Christ, Muslims in eternal bloody conflict with the invading Christian crusaders, Jews and Palestinians so deeply suspicious and resentful of each other that all they can do, most often disproportionately, is to hurt each other. When you identify yourself not as a vessel of God, a conduit through which the presence of the unified state can be felt to flow, but become entrenched instead in your *I*, you have to demonize *the other* in order to feel more secure in the artificially elevated status of your and your immediate community's false god, your *I* and the narrow beliefs *I* espouses.

Only one team ever wins the English Premier League. All the other teams are seen as vanquished and defeated and viewed as inferior. But God isn't some kind of soccer pitch with teams vying for supremacy, whose fans' allegiance can sometimes get whipped up into the passions of hooliganism. The felt presence of the unified state is not an attribute unique to you and your community and somehow superior to what your Jewish, Christian, or Muslim brothers and sisters might be feeling. It's a universal condition.

Regardless of our affiliation with the religion of our birth or choice, even if we have no affiliation, we're all children of the one God. We've all been born out of the unified state and will return there when we die. Imagine a world in which the practice of Breathing God heals not only the intense pain of our personal separation from God but the enmity among our religious siblings as well.

———◂▸———

I'm not trying
to make anything happen

I'm not trying
to manipulate anything
to change anything

I'm just breathing

this breath
now this one
and the breath itself
keeps revealing
all these new vistas
understandings
perspectives

don't strive for any kind of experience
just keep breathing

all I can do
is breathe
and let breath show me
whatever it will
both the obstacles to its free passage
through the conduit of my body
and the magnificent vistas that appear
when those obstacles fall away

The crack in the fabric of appearances that allows me to slip through into the felt embrace of union keeps opening and closing throughout the entire day. When I remember to remember my breath and yield to its potency, I lose myself but find God. When I forget to remember, the crack in the fabric closes, like a flower that closes at sunset, and once again I feel myself shut back in, separate from everything I can perceive to exist outside my body. All day long I pass in and out. All day long I remember my breath one moment and forget it the next. All day long the fissure in the fabric opens and shuts back down. Back and forth. Opening and closing. But I at least know where the secret pathway that lets me pass through into God is found. And with this understanding, I fall into sleep. Hopefully, I'll sleep better tonight.

Day Seven

Dark Nights in the Desert

When you throw a glass of water into the air on a frigidly cold night, the water splits apart into tens of thousands of individual ice crystals. That's what the Milky Way looks like out here in the desert. It's as though God went and spilled a carton of cosmic milk across the tabletop of the heavens. Whoever said stars were uniformly white must never have looked to the night sky in the desert. The stars are every color of the rainbow. Yes, many twinkle bright white, but others flicker red, blue, purple, yellow, green even. There goes a flashing meteor, flaming out as it streaks across the sky. Technically, it's day seven, but morning hasn't yet arrived. It's dark out. Moonless. And yet the stars are so bright that I can see the ground without having to worry about tripping.

Dawn is still many hours away, but there's no way I can sleep any longer. Something's happened, and I'm in a lot of pain. Residues of old illnesses that I remember from long ago have all returned. The back of my left leg burns, my head throbs. Every joint in my body is sore. My throat aches, not from cold or flu but from a pain that feels like someone has his hands gripped around my neck, is leering down at me, and won't let go. My mind's silence is long gone, hijacked by frantic thoughts of self-pity, misery, despair. Just yesterday I felt so close to God, bathed in a glowing flow of grace, but now . . . I feel I'm going to explode. I want to scream, cry out, push the pain away, but even if someone were to hear my cry, what could they do for me, really? I get out of bed, get dressed, and walk out into the dark night of the desert, where it strangely feels a more appropriate environment in which to be crushed.

my god
why have you forsaken me

is it heresy
great hubris and arrogance
even to say these words
to speak them for myself

but that's how i feel

the blessings and beatitudes of yesterday
are but distant memories today

i'm now swimming in an ocean of pain
i'm drowning there
why

Fleeing into the night doesn't relieve the pain and pressure, but it provides a far larger container for my pain to live, to just be. The four walls of my room felt claustrophobic. At least the desert sky is big enough to receive me as I am. Every few minutes I start to shake.

Later in the day, I look back on what happened and try to make some sense of it all:

The path to God through the medium of the breath is not a simple or straight one. It curves, it takes unexpected detours and reroutings, it showers me with grace one moment and strings me up on hooks the next, taunting me for my foolishness in thinking that grace once found can never again be lost, that breath once found can never again be shut down. The path of surrendering to breath ebbs and flows, and it's during its passage through darkness—where breath is lost and can't be located, where body hurts and emotions run ragged—that I'm tested and, let's be honest, usually found lacking. The hubris is not in crying out to God. The hubris is in thinking that, once brought to awareness, the breath will never leave me or that there will never be further sediments of separation I will have to deal with, engage, and heal through.

And then there is this hopeful vision of what was transpiring:

This cycling back and forth between the beatitude of God's grace and the descent back down into freshly emerging residues of pain isn't a confirming sign that things have gone badly off the rails. It's the opposite, really. Like it or not (not), I'm right on track. It's how the path of breath proceeds—

smooth one moment, lurching the next. The path doesn't just jerk me back
and forth but moves me forward along the trajectory of an upward spiral.
If I wasn't supposed to feel this deep level of ache, why would I be feeling it?

I know that the way through pain is to accept it as it is and
keep breathing, but it's really hard to do. It would be so easy to
just shut breath back down, go unconscious, hope for the best
in the morning. But if I were to run from it—out of touch, out
of mind—wouldn't I just be confronted by it again, tomorrow
or the next day? So I soldier on.

———◄►———

Breath is a purifier and a healer and sometimes a rough lover.
It doesn't just soothe and coddle and cradle. Yes, there's great
joy when I feel my mind melt away into the bliss of God's presence, but that blessed moment doesn't last forever. Layer by layer,
breath takes me down into the center of my center, revealing forgotten joys and darkened spiderwebs both. It's almost as though
the purpose of the beautiful bright openings is to allow the next
darkened layers of sensation and memory to come out.

The path of Breathing God dredges long-repressed pain,
anger, sadness, and guilt up to the surface, where I either ride
along with them, letting them eventually release their sickening
grip, or shove them back down. I completely understand why
we don't want anything to do with their reemergence, but if you
don't face them head-on, you remain at their mercy, affected by
them forever. Either way, it's a bad choice to have to make.

I may love the ecstatic openings as superficial personas

fade and release, exposed to the cleansing power of the breath. But as much as I love the openings, that's how much the pain of the next layer hurts.

> *like peeling back*
> *the layers of an onion*
>
> *you peel away a dry layer*
> *and the onion radiates*
> *a translucent glow*
> *fresh*
> *moist*
> *vibrant with life*
>
> *two days later*
> *having sat out on the counter*
> *the radiance is gone*
> *the watery shine turns opaque*
> *the glow darkens*
> *and the next layer is now ready*
> *to be peeled back and away*

It's critical on this path to understand this natural cycling of light turning dark, then light again, of bliss exposing deeper pain that resolves itself into deeper bliss, of layers of grace revealing deeper holdings, deeper resistances to both God and the breath. Without this understanding, it's all too easy to be so disheartened that you'll want to stop all this silly business, make excuses as to why this isn't working, conclude that God, the unified state, isn't for you. Even with this understanding, you'll be disheartened because that's what dark nights do.

───◄►───

The mind, with its thoughts and its sovereign "I," will do its absolute best to keep the presence of God away, to block God's entrance into the sacred crucible of the human body, for it knows that the appearance of God's presence, the unified state, can only occur in conjunction with its shutting off. One of the mind's most effective preservational strategies—if it can tell we're getting serious about seeing through its veils—is to expose us to the storehouse of pain that's mostly kept under wraps when we restrict our breath. When we begin the practice of Breathing God, it's not just the grace and shimmer and feelings of universal love that come to the surface of the body. It's the residues of pain, anger, fear, depression, insatiable cravings, and hardened aversions as well, and all of these hurt. The reemergence of all the feelings we've stuffed down and held back, the coming face-to-face with all the attitudes that have kept us apart from God hurts, and this hurt is generally more than enough to keep us from ever going anywhere near it.

Jacob wrestles with an unseen angel. Jesus confronts the tempters of darkness. Muhammad must have returned from the mountain exhausted from his efforts. Rumi enters into a period of unbearable grief and heartache when his great friend Shams, with whom he feels joined in spirit as one, just ups and leaves. It's easy to embrace the practice of Breathing God when all is going swimmingly, when the body begins to light up and

lighten up, to shimmer with the felt glow of incoming presence, when breath touches into the whole of the body, touching into every cell. But it becomes far more challenging when
the shimmer reveals the next viscous layer of darkness, and
pain and doubt come rushing forward. But I keep repeating to
myself, over and over, like a mantra of hope:

> *there's never been a dark night*
> *that doesn't eventually end*
> *there's never been a dark night*
> *that doesn't eventually end*
> *there's never been a dark night*
> *that doesn't eventually end*

Dawn is advertised as always coming, and here's where faith
and belief are relevant and legitimate companions to practices
that rely only on direct experience. We need to trust in the
wisdom of the body's healing process, the knowledge that this
too shall pass, because without this understanding and faith,
there's no way we'd proceed further, right into and through
the jaws of darkness. And even though, in those moments of
darkness when I cry out, "My God, why have you forsaken
me?" I'm determined to continue on, breath after breath, until
the dark night lifts. I don't really have much choice.

———◄►———

God plays a constant game of hide-and-seek, now appearing,
now disappearing, just like subatomic particles that emerge

into existence for the briefest moment before disappearing back into a formless state that we have little understanding of or direct access to. I know it's important to accept the cyclic nature of God's emergences and disappearances, but when breath thrusts me into a dark night of anguish, it's hard to accept it joyfully. It's hard for me even to breathe as I sit in my room after breakfast. My chest is wrapped in a constricting vest of pain. I feel like a car that's getting crushed for scrap. Pain is painful. It hurts. I have to do something. But what?

Later in the morning, still in the grip of the predawn assault, I decide to go to the chapel for one of the many prayer gatherings that occur throughout the Benedictines' day. Any harbor in a storm, and if there's solace in prayer, I'm open to receiving it. Besides, I know the Benedictines' prayer services are quite beautiful, and a dose of beauty, even if only a distraction, may be just what a doctor of the soul might order for me (or so I hope). What's so glorious about the Benedictines' services is that they don't speak their prayers; they sing them. Psalms are set to music and sung with simple slow melody lines that float above the soft healing sound of a synthesized organ.

I sit in the chapel. I follow the hymnal. I listen to the words during the soothing recitation of the morning's passage, and—as hard as this is for me to believe at first—I hear an answer! It comes from Psalm 119, the longest psalm in the Old Testament, whose words are sometimes attributed to the great Jewish king David himself:

> *in the night, Lord,*
> *I remember your name*
> *that I may keep your law*

Hearing this passage, I have a revelation. In a flashing moment of recognition, I realize that a solution for how to traverse the dark night, whose spell I'm still under, may have just been shown to me. Remembering your name. Remembering your name in the dark night. How do I best remember to remember God's name? How? By listening to my breath.

Hearing these words catapults me into a whole new awareness of breath that I end up exploring for the rest of the day and into the beginning of the next as well. A full, deep breath is rarely silent. It makes a sibilant sound entering and leaving my body, especially when I'm breathing through my mouth, and through that sound I start to hear the name of God. Remembering God's name, actually hearing myself call out to God on every breath, becomes the life raft that—as crazy an idea as this might be, but I don't have any other ideas—I hope will shepherd me across the ocean of my distress. Through every breath I take, I call out to God. I remember his name.

◄—►

The unified state goes by many names. Call what happens God if you like. Call it the *mahamudric* ground state if you prefer. Call it the Great Wide Open. Call it the implicate order that the quantum physicist David Bohm saw as the source dimension out of which all matter, all physical form, is projected. Call it the freeing of yourself from the misperceptions of Plato's cave. Call it the nondual state, the monotheistic truth. The name is ultimately not important, and for many Jews even the utterance of the name out loud is considered sacrilegious, but I'm not uttering any name. All I'm doing is surrendering to the breath, one after the other, yielding to its potency, its healing love, entering into the beatitude, however you decide to name it, and listening to what it sounds like.

Breathing God's Names

as you breathe in deeply
as you breathe out fully
especially in the silence of the desert
your breath makes a sound
and this sound
is the name of god

on every breath you take
call out to god
to help you traverse the night
of darkness and despair
just as the psalm directs you to

for many jews
uttering god's name
as a word
is considered heresy
for how can god
be reduced to a word

but breathing in deeply
breathing out fully
you can hear god's name

not as a word
but as the sound of your breath

breathing in a sound like yah
breathing out a sound like way
hearing god's name
on every cycle of breath
yah . . . way
yah . . .way
yah . . . way
no word
no name
just the sound of breath

the muslim
during zikr
breathes the name
of allah
on every breath
he or she takes

breathing in a sound like ah
breathing out a sound like lah
remembering god's name
in every cycle of breath
ah . . . lah
ah . . . lah
ah . . . lah
no word

no name
just the sound of breath

the christian
during prayer
can breathe the name of jesus
on every breath
he or she takes

breathing in a sound like hay
breathing out a sound like su
remembering god's name
on every cycle of breath
hay . . . su
hay . . . su
hay . . . su
no word
no name
just the sound of breath

All languages invent words to describe sounds.

oink oink goes the pig
bowwow says the dog

but oink is not the sound
that comes from the pig's mouth
neither is bowwow

the sound a dog makes

the word is not the thing

And so also do humans make nonlinguistic sounds that we nonetheless transpose into language. We place our tongue against our upper palate just behind our teeth, feel the suction of its contact, squeeze it, then draw it away quickly and forcibly, often twice in a row, and out comes a sound that signals disapproval or annoyance. We may write this as *tsk tsk*, but the sound that we make has nothing to do with those written words or their pronunciation as *tisk tisk*.

And so it is with the names of God. *God* is not a word we utter through our language but a sound that appears on our breath. On every breath we take, we can hear the name of God. We can remember the name of God. With every breath we take, we can call out to God. And breath speaks in a universal language, no matter what your native tongue is. There's no more Tower of Babel in the breath.

I leave the chapel and spend the rest of the day breathing God's names:

> *yah . . . way*
> *yah . . . way*
> *yah . . .way*
>
> *ah . . . lah*
> *ah . . . lah*
> *ah . . . lah*

hay . . . su

hay . . . su

hay . . . su

Yahweh, Allah, Jesus . . . Yahweh, Allah, Jesus. I've always felt ecumenically allegiant to all three of the great monotheistic religions, so I cycle through them all. I spend an hour intoning *yah . . . way*. I spend another hour breathing *ah . . . lah*. I shift the sound of my breath, ever so slightly, to *hay . . . su*. I don't say *yahway, ahlah, haysu*. I just listen and hear those sounds in my breath. Breathing in through my mouth, I hear a sound like *yah, ah, hay*. Breathing out through my mouth I hear a sound like *way, lah, su*. The inhalations through my mouth are long and full. God's names are right there, right upon my breath.

I call out and listen to God's names, over and over and over again, and it works, as I finally transition out of my dark night back into a brighter day. By afternoon I feel recovered from whatever had happened to me, the bout of intense discomfort I went through last night. By evening I'm floating again on God's breath, feeling God enter my entire body on the inhalation, dying back into God's great expanse on the exhalation, at times even feeling God entering not just the physical limbs of my body but everything I can see and hear as well, on every inhalation, floating on my surrendered breath, breathing in, breathing out, the dark night now past even as I lie down on my bed, feeling exhausted from the ordeal of the long day that started in the darkness of the early morning, falling off into a light but peaceful sleep.

Living on Air,
God Breathes Me

half asleep
half awake
the distinction between
what's dream
what's not
not at all clear
god's names still riding on my breath

yah . . . way
ah . . . lah
hay . . . su

calling out to god
all through the night
feeling the sound of god's names
vibrating through my body
gliding effortlessly

a dream person floating
right through the secret passageway
into the waiting arms
of god's embrace
the land of felt union

no more distinction
between inner and outer
just union
inner and outer commingling
everything in the room
somehow a part of me
the visual field
no longer something out there
but something in here
right in the very center
of me

As I transition out of sleep, God's names still sounding on my breath, conceptual distinctions, like cooped-up birds seeking release, are flying out the window into the early glow of first light. Inner/outer . . . body/mind . . . self/other . . . I can't even honestly discern a whole lot of difference between what's breath and what's body. That's how merged and mixed up everything's getting.

breath is the invisible reflection
of the body's form
body is breath made visible

This is especially obvious when breath stimulates sensation in every cell of my body, but it's just as true when breath gets held back and restrained. When breath becomes constricted and shallow, so also does the feeling presence of body remain shut down and unfelt. Out of touch, thought proliferates and fills up the space that silent presence and the fields of vision and sound can otherwise occupy.

> *unfelt body*
> *restricted breath*
>
> *awakened body*
> *breathing god*

I find myself following along a questionable path of circular logic (A begets B, B begets C—so C begets A?): When we shut down the breath we lose touch with a feeling presence. Doing this causes random, unbidden thoughts to arise in the mind, which in turn keeps the breath shut. And the shutting of the breath further feeds thoughts that . . .

I'm concerned that this journal is starting to take on a nonlinear logic. Bringing breath to life kindles the feeling presence of the body, but the reverse is also true. If I focus not on breath but on body, shifting my attention from thoughts to feeling presence, breath becomes softer, fuller, more regular, more expansive. So which comes first? The chicken of the breath or the body of the egg? Yes, that's what I just wrote. See what I mean about nonlinear logic?

I'm relieved that I slept OK last night but still feel shaken from the events of yesterday. Whatever got dredged up from the dark corners of my mind and body was so hard to just be with and breathe into, a putrescence of pain and anger, fear and sorrow leaking from me, like a boil that comes to the surface and just sits there and festers before it eventually pops. And even though I know in my mind that I have to accept and yield to whatever breath serves up next, it's only human not to like it. And is there something, anything, I can do to make sure that the boil's been lanced and the crisis of yesterday is over, at least for now?

The best way I've always known to stop feeding the residues of physical ache that won't let go, the waves of emotional distress when they engulf me, the proliferation of thought that swarms me, the distance from God that bedevils me, the healing of the surfacing of impurities . . . is to stop taking food, so I decide to fast today.

When I first started reading spiritual literature in my early twenties, I was initially drawn to a book about the Essenes called *The Essene Gospel of Peace* by Edmund Bordeaux Szekely. The Essenes were a Jewish sect from the time of Jesus who lived apart, away from the crowded city clusters, out in the countryside by lakes and streams. The Essenes of two thousand years ago sounded to me like a biblical version of the back-to-the-land hippies of the 1960s and 1970s. They removed themselves, as best they could, from the political turmoil of their times and chose to align their lives more closely with the energies and rhythms of nature. To this end, they regularly engaged in purification practices, removing the residues of city life from their body and mind, through periodic fasting and internal cleansing. I might as well have been reading about contemporary figures like Bernard Jensen or Stanley Burroughs, seminal figures in the natural healing movement in the West.

This was at a time in my life when I was trying to sort out my relationship with the religion of my birth, and in the Essenes I found a Judaism that I could wholeheartedly embrace. I began experimenting with juice fasting and colon cleansing and found that, as challenging as they were, I loved how they affected me. After successfully completing a seven- or ten-day cleanse, I inevitably would feel physically as well as emotionally lighter, uplifted, purified. Much of the residual ache in the tissues of my body would be relieved, things that I was worried about or was grappling with emotionally had lifted, and the opaque barriers separating me from God felt far more translucent. Fasting was like a great, altogether natural drug that left me feeling intoxicated, in direct contact with my higher instincts. I couldn't really call it an altered state, as the high that I was feeling felt completely natural, in fact far more natural than what I would ordinarily feel when I wasn't fasting.

Hunger was rarely a challenge for me as, within a few hours, I'd start feeling far more vibratory and alive. The challenge was when the cleanse started bringing impurities to the surface, and I would undergo long hours, sometimes days, of what's known as a *healing crisis* in which my head and body ached, my belly felt twisted, and I'd watch my mood plummet. During such a crisis it also felt as though the energy in my body had been sapped, like water draining from a sink, and all I could effectively do was lie down and rest or take a warm Epsom salt bath. At night I'd administer an enema, and once I got used to the weirdness of bathing my colon, I found it helped enormously in relieving the ache and settling out the emotions.

So this morning I thought it would be a good idea to abstain from solid foods for the entire day and just drink water. I'd clearly gone through some kind of healing crisis yesterday, and the best way I could think to make sure that whatever had surfaced was moving out of my body and mind was to switch my routine to purification mode. So I decided to fast. No food. Just water. Little physical exertion.

All three of the Abrahamic religions, to a greater or lesser degree, include periods of fasting in which you abstain from food as a way of seeking forgiveness for things you may have done that hurt others. Jews abstain from all food and water on Yom Kippur, their day of atonement, when they think back over the year to all the things they wished they could have done differently. Even though they aren't required to give up all solid food, Christians eat more lightly during Lent, especially on Ash Wednesday and Good Friday, as a way of reflecting on the forty days and nights Jesus went without food in the desert. During the month of Ramadan, Muslims world-wide abstain from taking any solid food and water during the daylight hours.

Although fasting as a religious observance is often considered an act of penance, it can also be explored in a more broadly mystical context as a way of healing the body, silencing the mind, settling out emotions, and drawing closer to the palpable felt presence of God. Nowhere is this combination of physical, mental, emotional, and spiritual cleansing advocated more clearly than in the spontaneously uttered poetry of the Islamic mystic Rumi who loved to fast because fasting, he would say—just as it's always done for me—would get him very high, his heart cleaner, his soul clearer, the presence of God nearer:

> *we've cleaned our heart and soul with*
> > *fasting*
> *the dirt that's been with us*
> *has been washed away now*

> *fasting causes some inevitable stress*
> *but the invisible treasure of the heart*
> > *gets revealed*

> *fasting is wine for the soul*
> *and gets you very drunk*

> *drink the wine of eternity*
> *give up eating and drinking*
> *be full without food*

when you're fasting
you're the guest of god
and are served the meal of heaven

if you take fasting to heart
you'll hear a voice
i am at your service
i am at your service
every time you call out
"o my god"

The Benedictines at this monastery eat well. Throughout my stay I've been on my own for an early, light breakfast, which usually consists of fruit, tea and toast, and a choice of cereals and nut butters. Lunches and dinners are sit-down affairs in the large dining hall with long tables at which a dozen or more people can comfortably sit. At lunch we sit at our table and, after opening prayers, are served our food on large platters by several of the young monks. One of the tenets of the Benedictine order is to treat everyone you meet as Christ, and the young monks are especially radiant in their serving of food. At one meal a monk seated at a table far across the hall from me saw that I'd forgotten to pour myself a glass of water. He broke off his meal to get up, fetch a glass, pour water, and bring it over to me, almost apologetic that I'd overlooked getting water for myself and he hadn't noticed it immediately.

At dinner we walk through a line and serve ourselves with leftovers from lunch. The food is abundant and delicious:

beans, salads, multiple servings of vegetables, homemade bread, jams and nut butters, fish or chicken, occasional desserts. It's an all-you-can-eat affair, with the monks returning again and again to your table at lunch with their platters of food and the buffet at dinner open as many times as you like.

But today I go nowhere near the dining hall. Just water. All day long. I don't start feeling the first pangs of hunger until the late morning but find that sensations of hunger, if not given into but breathed into instead, start changing their effect and turn increasingly vibratory, a shimmering of life force, an alchemical turning of lead into gold:

> *food is our culture's*
> *addictive drug of choice*
>
> *letting my obsession with food go*
> *makes it that much easier*
> *just to be with my breath*
> *no distractions*
> *just letting go*
> *breath by breath*

I spend most of the day lying on my bed, breath going in, breath going out, and by the afternoon—as my mind becomes less sluggish, my body more vibratory—it feels less like I'm breathing than being breathed. It's not the conventional *me* initiating my breath any longer. The breath just breathes me. It fills and empties my lungs, my body, but I'm not doing it.

There's no effort on my part. The breath just breathes. I fast because I'm hungry for God's presence and no longer, at least for the moment, fearful of the potency of that presence.

What we call the fear of God is mirrored in the fear we have of letting go into the deep sensations of the body, surrendering to the current of the life force that wants to burst through us like a flash flood in a desert, surrendering to the force of breath that wants to remind us of God in every inhalation we take, every exhalation we make. We begin by breathing God into and out of our bodies, but as we keep surrendering to this mightiest of forces and impulses, we get to a place where the body simply becomes an open conduit through which the force of God, in the form of the inhalation and exhalation of breath, passes right through, essentially breathing us.

> *i'm but a conduit*
> *through which the presence of god*
> *passes through me*
> *and in this way*
> *i do my part*
> *in bringing god to earth*

Rumi tells us that bringing breath to life is the essence of every truly religious act, for when we bring breath to life, we bring God to Earth. What would you do if you knew that God was coming to your home as a guest and was going to spend the weekend with you? Wouldn't you clean the room God would be staying in, making it as fresh, as tidy, as free of dirt and clutter as you possibly could? Wouldn't you scrub the floors so they shine?

your body is the room
that god enters and exits
with every breath you take

can you prepare the room of your body
making it fit for god to inhabit
with the same spic and span
with which you'd prepare
the room in your home
for a very special guest

fasting cleans the interior
of the room of your body
in much the same way
as a hot shower
cleans the exterior
of the room of your body
after a hard day's labor

fasting removes
the impediments to breath

all day long
living on air
breath after breath
god feeds me
invisible food

Breath is more verb than noun. It's a process more than a thing. It's invisible, but you can feel it, like a breeze that blows and cools you on a hot summer's night. It's constantly changing every moment, turning out the next, turning back in again, never ever standing completely still, stopping only when you pass over into your death. It moves you. It wants free passage through the conduit of your God-created body, such a sacred offering, such an extraordinary opportunity. Fasting makes it easier to remember how to surrender to this force of God. Do I resist this force? Or do I let go to it? And how do I resist it and let go to it?

As the sky darkens and the colors turn, I feel the need to sleep. Yesterday's nightmare is over and gone. I rest on my back. I'm back in God's breath. When I don't stuff my belly with food, it becomes so much easier to breathe. I fall asleep tonight with an empty belly but a full heart.

Day Nine

Walking in God's Footsteps

Waking up to the first faint suggestion of light, I don't want to leave my bed. And so I don't. I just let myself lie there under the warmth of the thick covers and turn my attention to my breath. I become aware of it. I start feeling it. I start letting go to it. And I even start seeing it. The desert can get as cold on a cloudless night as it gets sweltering during the day with the sun bearing down. Last night was very cold, but still I left my window open to enjoy the fresh crispness of the cool desert air. As I lie in bed, peeking up out of the heavy duvet that kept my body warm during the night, I can see my breath every time I exhale as a cloudy, swirling mist leaving my body.

Mostly I've been exploring Breathing God either lying down in bed, sitting up in a chair in the posture of the Egyptian pharaohs, or sitting cross-legged on meditation cushions on the floor. The most prolonged passages of breath awareness—during which my mind stays relatively empty and I feel God close by—occur when my body isn't moving around too much. As soon as I stand up and start moving about—

to the guesthouse's washroom, on a walk in the gardens, up to the monastery for a meal, or to participate in the chanted prayers—it becomes much more difficult to stay with my breath, to let it breathe into me and have the presence of God replace the silent chitterings and chatterings of my mind that broadcast the fake news that separation is the only perspective from which I can interact with the world. Every time I go for a walk, it seems I become less filled with grace (less graceful?) and contract back down again into the thoughts in my head. Why is this? And what can I do about it?

> *i want to be with my breath*
> *not just when i'm sitting or lying down*
> *but when i'm standing and moving*
>   *about as well*
>
> *i want to do my best*
> *to follow the path of the upright*
> *and walk in god's footsteps*
>
> *even though*
> *a relative immobility*
> *appears to support*
> *my surrender to breath*
> *i know that god's here*
> *all the time*

I'm also nearing the end of my retreat, and I haven't explored the magnificent desert valley that drew the Benedictines to found and build a monastery here. I've taken short walks down to the river and walked along its edge . . .

One day, a tour group of kayakers comes floating past where I'm walking. "What a stunningly gorgeous day!" exclaims a middle-aged man, lying back on the seat of his kayak, beaming, his palms out to his side, his arms moving up and down in a gesture of awe. "What an amazing valley." I put my palms together and bring them to my heart. "It's perfect," I say and bow to him with a large smile, remembering how the Benedictines view everyone they encounter as a manifestation of Christ.

. . . and several times a day I've walked the half mile or so to take my meals, back and forth on the dirt road connecting the guesthouse to the monastery, but I still haven't ventured outside the margins of the monastery grounds and let myself wander out along the paths and trails that lead into narrow canyons or out onto the valley floor.

And one of the reasons for this is that, when I walk, I tend to contract back down into my thoughts and weaken my direct, felt connection with God. Again, the question asks itself, why? So after breakfast I fill up my water bottle, put on my hiking sandals, place some energy bars in a fanny pack that I buckle around my waist, apply sunscreen, put on a hat and sunglasses, and set out into the desert to see if I can find out why . . . and to do something about it.

The first thing I notice, as I walk through the wooden gate of the guesthouse and start moving along the dirt road that winds and dips for thirteen miles until it reaches the main asphalt highway, is that I tend to look down at the ground when I walk. OK. This is understandable in that I have to make sure that that there's nothing in my way that's going to trip me up. But to be always looking down, I have to bring tension into my head and neck, and I remember back to the fourth day of the retreat when I discovered what stiffening my neck and holding my head still did to me. With my head bent forward, out in front of the rest of my body, I have to contract the muscles in my upper back to keep my head from falling off, my head from falling off, my head from falling off . . .

"Off with his head!" cried the Queen of Hearts in Alice in Wonderland. Might she have been speaking of people whose heads are so far out in front of the vertical axis of their upright body that they lose their felt connection with God and get compressed down into their thoughts so that the only way to free them from their imprisonment in their minds is to chop off their heads?

. . . and toppling even farther toward the ground were I truly to relax that tension. If I'm to feel uplifted, gracefully drawn up toward God, doesn't my head have to rise back up where it belongs, where it can float on top of my shoulders while I'm walking, where it can bob along like a fishing bobber on the waves of a lake over which a breeze is blowing?

the red red robin
goes bob bob bobbin' along

———▶———

The next thing I notice is that when I focus my gaze so narrowly on the ground in front of my feet, I lose sight of the whole visual field. I only see what I want to see and disregard everything else, like a hawk flying over the desert floor looking for a little mole to eat. As soon as I block out anything in any of my primary sensory fields—sensation, vision, sound—I fall back down into my mind, my thoughts, my sense of separation, and God disappears. And so I start to walk more slowly. I don't just focus my attention on any one object in front of me. Instead, I pay attention to the peripheries of the visual field, everything that softly appears out at the right and left sides of my elliptical field of vision. I immediately like how staying simultaneously aware of the right and left edges of my visual field affects me. The energies in the right and left sides of my head become more balanced, I become more present, and viewing the whole of the visual field becomes more natural. (Might this be what Jesus meant by looking out onto the world with *single vision?*)

When I see the whole field all at once rather than any one thing in particular, I can still stay alert to objects in the near distance that might want to trip me. When I get closer to them, I look down briefly, walk around them, and then immediately let my vision go once again wide and inclusive. The more I walk like this, the better I get at it so that, by the afternoon, I can glide around obstacles that I viewed many seconds earlier without having to break off seeing the entire visual field all at once and looking down.

> *keeping vision wide*
> *letting myself see*
> *way over on the left*
> *way over on the right*
> *focusing on the peripheries*
> *i see everything*
> *all at once*

———◄—►———

The next thing I notice is that I'm walking like a stick figure. My arms don't move much, my hips don't sway much, my legs move forward as though I've got cross-country skis on and am skiing along parallel tracks that have been carved into the snow. Some parts of my body move, others don't, and I remember back to a gospel song I sang in my high school glee club . . .

> *toe bone connected to the foot bone*
> *foot bone connected to the heel bone*
> *heel bone connected to the ankle bone*
> *ankle bone connected to the . . .*
>
> *now hear the word of the lord*

. . . where I learned my first important lesson about the body: everything's connected. You can't isolate one part from another. What happens in one part of the body directly affects every other part.

But as I walk along the dirt road, I realize I'm not just one of the stiff-necked people. I'm one of the stiff-bodied people! And if God was none too pleased about his children's stiff necks, what would he have to say about stiff bodies?

And so I stop. And stand. I turn my attention back to my breath. There it is again. Breathing in, breathing out. I relax and gradually start feeling my whole body come back alive as felt presence, toe bone to head bone. I look out on the magnificent valley in front of me. I listen to the birds calling out as they scamper back and forth from one small tree to another. I start moving. And I fall through the crack in the fabric of the world's appearances and dissolve back into the felt presence of God.

Since the only constant in our world is that everything is changing, in a state of eternal flux, I know I can't hold on to this holy moment. But I also want to figure out how I needn't leave it completely behind as I start walking. And the gospel song starts singing itself again inside my head that's connected to my neck bone that's connected to everything else in my body. What it's telling me—*now hear the word of the Lord!*—is that if I want to stay connected to the feeling state of God's presence while I'm walking, I need to make sure, as my legs keep propelling me forward along the path, that everything else in my body can be felt to respond to those motions. Everything. Like a chain reaction of movement where a cue stick strikes a billiard ball that strikes another billiard ball that strikes . . .

My first lesson in transmitted motion happened as a child growing up on a lake in Minnesota. I'd skate out onto the frozen lake on a winter's night with several of my friends. We'd join hands together in a line and skate ahead as fast as we could. Then, suddenly, without warning, the designated skater on one of the far ends of the line would stop suddenly, and everyone would get spun around to shouts of glee and the occasional tumble.

Motion initiated anywhere can be transmitted through the entire body, one joint to the next to the next. So that a leg moving forward can initiate a chain of motion that—click, click, click, passing from one joint to the next—eventually reaches the head and causes it to bob and move in response, the entire body constantly moving, nothing staying still, nothing resisting the wave-like motion that wants to be transmitted through it. Most animals move with a coordinated grace throughout their body. Why can't I?

So I start experimenting with keeping my entire body in loose, resilient motion as I move along the dirt road. My hips sway; my arms swing; my head doesn't just look straight ahead but bobs back and forth, like an upside-down *u*. Following the direction of the leg that's moving forward, my body rotates to the right and left around the vertebra in my spine where my lower thoracic torso meets my upper lumbar torso, right shoulder going back as right leg goes forward, back and forth, back and forth, everything moving. And even though analyzing this is starting to feel like the caterpillar explaining how he walks, God starts speaking to me again in the silent language of felt presence.

albert einstein
in a letter to his son

life is like riding a bicycle
to stay in balance
everything has to keep moving

Like a tightrope walker on a rope, I can walk with elegance and grace. If I can play with the same kind of upright balance that allows giant sequoia trees, Gothic spires, and modern skyscrapers to rise up into the sky, gravity can actually be felt to support and buoy me up, and in this state of relaxed, literally uplifted grace, my entire body moves on each step and breath.

As I keep moving ahead—breathing, feeling, seeing, hearing, everything moving, joyous—I inevitably come to a place, maybe it's just a thought about how joyous this new way of walking is, where I suddenly find myself back in my head, back in my thoughts. And as soon as I wake up again to this compression, caused by sinking back down into thinking, I realize that something somewhere in my body has stopped moving. Maybe my shoulders have gone still. Maybe my hips have quit swaying. Certainly, my head and neck have stiffened. Somewhere. So thought after thought, I turn my attention back to my body, find out where I've gone still, and start letting everything move again.

I walk out into the desert. It's easier to walk with this kind of dancerly grace and motion when I have confidence in the ground underneath my feet and the path I'm walking along, when the way is broad and flat with no rocks or pebbles, no sticks or branches, no roots or bushes. When I have this kind of confidence, my head can look ahead, not just down at the ground, bobbing left and right, up and down, and take in the whole of the visual field all at once. I don't fix my gaze on any one object. By focusing on the whole of the visual field, rather than darting my gaze here to there, I don't bring a stiffening of tension into my eyes, which are connected to my head bone connected to my neck bone connected to my . . . and so I can move, really move, along the desert floor without abandoning God.

As soon as I feel once again lost in thought, I stop for a moment . . .

> *i remember*
> *my mother's words to me*
> *about what to do*
> *when i get to an intersection in the road*
> *on my way to school*
>
> *stop*
> *look*
> *listen*

. . . gather myself, tune in again to the felt presence of my body and breath, play with the dance of upright balancing . . .

there's no such thing as standing still
whenever i come to standing
and truly let myself relax
surrendering to gravity's pull
while feeling drawn up toward the stars
everything sways and moves

. . . soften my eyes that, lost in thought, narrow down to focus on but a single object, broaden my gaze to see the whole of the roughly elliptical visual field all at once, open my ears to hear everything that's here to be heard, relax into motion. And suddenly I have God back. Felt breathing body merges with the visual field. Sounds start commingling with body and vision. Breath breathes through everything: my entire body, the whole of the visual field, all the sounds. Breath and motion are the glue that binds these three primary fields, which ordinarily speak to me so loudly of separation, back into the unified presence of God.

Listen, children of God, everything is of one piece. So says the *shema*, the primary prayer of Jewish faith. God is the one, not the many. Not just for Jews, but for Muslims and Christians, for all of God's children. We may all call the one God by different names, but it's still the same thing, the same presence, the same feeling state.

Sometimes I'm able to walk with this grace for a minute at a time before thought once again breaks in, like a thief in the night, without my being aware, and steals away my felt presence, my commingled awareness of breath, body, vision, sound. Sometimes I can only take a step or two before I realize that God's withdrawn again. I know God is always here, but I don't just want to know he's here. I want to feel him or her or it or whatever. I want to feel him walking with me, as me, in my footsteps, in his footsteps.

One path takes me to the river, across a bridge, and beyond through fields of juniper, cactus, and flowering shrubs. Another takes me into a canyon along a dry streambed, the walls on either side of the stream narrowing, narrowing farther, until I come to a sacred spot where the two walls meet, and I can't go any farther. I can hear the song of the birds at the far end of the canyon. Their voices sound magnified, as though they're singing their songs through miniature megaphones. I can hear my breath, from the exertion of the walk, as an echo bouncing off the narrow canyon walls. I walk much more slowly than I ordinarily do, and this helps me not lose my expanded awareness of the whole of the visual field, the feeling presence of my body, the symphony of sounds. I just keep moving. And breathing.

At the end of the day, I make my way back to the guesthouse, take a hot shower, swaying in the shower, put fresh clothes on, and walk back up to the monastery for evening prayers and dinner. The notes of the sung prayers move up and down the scale. The fingers of the organist move from key to key. We live in a universe in which everything moves. Nothing stands still, not even for a little minute. At dinner I lift my fork to my mouth and feel this simple motion transmitting itself throughout my loose body, rocking me softly in my chair. Rock my soul in the bosom of Abraham. I walk back to my room, and before the darkness of the desert night has pushed the last light of day aside, I fall into a deep sleep, breathing in, breathing out, the breath never coming to rest, never standing still.

Dreams of Peace

*I*n the middle of the night I'm awakened by a coyote's piercing cry, at once so human and otherworldly. This must be, I think, the flute of Kokopelli, the mythical trickster spirit of the American Southwest, summoning all God's children back to him, a pied piper in moccasins and feathers. I listen. The coyote cries again, not mournful, not supplicating, just a cry letting you know that there are spirits about. It cries again. Do you hear me? it asks. And, if you hear me, well . . . Are you going to keep on resisting, as you always have, holding back on your opportunity for freedom, or are you going to come and seek me out? Are you going to follow my cry, and let me take you where you most want to go? Come, follow me.

It cries again, a long series of notes. Aoouuuahooo, heeeahh, heeaiahh. No human voice, no human flute, can make such a sound. I rise from my bed, put on my clothes, and walk out into the desert night.

I orient myself by the stars and the moon. The coyote's cry is coming from the east, from where the sun will rise in just a few hours and a new day will begin. The full moon lights my way, and I'm able to walk out into the desert night, through the piñon and juniper trees, past the ocotillo cactus, without fear of stumbling or losing my footing. I keep moving in *the direction of the coyote's song, summoning me farther, deeper, as it leads me into a canyon recess. The walls of the canyon narrow, and I keep on walking until I can reach out and touch the canyon walls with both my hands. I think to myself: Is this the end of the path or just the beginning? I wait and listen. And then I hear the coyote once again, calling to me. Don't stop now, it's saying. Look. Over to your left. Find the small crevice in the canyon wall, and keep walking. Come, follow me.*

I squeeze myself through a narrow passage, and suddenly a whole new canyon appears before me, a beautiful, deep canyon bathed in moonlight, with sheer cliffs rising on all sides and a waterfall in the far distance. I come to a river and am suddenly on the other side. The canyon just keeps getting larger and larger. I listen for the coyote's song to guide me farther, but the coyote has gone silent. The river and waterfall have disappeared. I'm bathed in silence, and the night has gone suddenly dark. I stop and rest and wonder what I'm to do and where I'm to go next.

I hear a shuffling on the canyon floor, look over to my right, and see the jackrabbit. Its ears are very large, and its nose is quivering in the cool desert night. It looks up at me with great compassion and tenderness . . . and winks! Ah, I get it. You're my new guide, and I follow the jackrabbit as it scurries away behind a stand of juniper trees. It keeps turning and looking back at me, making sure I'm following in its steps. The moon comes out from behind the cover of a cloud, and the canyon is once again bathed in light. The rabbit leads me along a rocky escarpment into yet another canyon. As I round another corner, it looks up at me one last time and is gone.

And then I see the figures sheltered under a piñon tree. There are three of them, men, old men with beards, huddled together on a blanket or rug. And in a startling moment of recognition, I realize that it's Jesus, Moses, and Muhammad. Moses is very old. He looks so frail and is sitting to my left on the rug, wrapped in warm blankets with a monk's cowl covering his head. Muhammad is kneeling next to him. He has a bowl of warm soup or warm milk in his hands and is tenderly feeding Moses with a wooden spoon. Moses leans his head toward the offering and takes the nourishing liquid a slow spoonful at a time. Jesus is standing behind them both. He has his arms wrapped around them to add comfort and warmth. He's smiling softly. His head is slowly moving back and forth between them. First, I see him bring his head to Moses's head. Then he moves it over to Muhammad's head. Back and forth he moves his head, touching and embracing them, head to head, cheek to cheek.

I'm back at the river. The sound of the flowing water over the rocky bottom is mesmerizing. I want to listen to it forever. I look over and see a small child. I can't tell if it's a young boy or girl. The child has a cup and is drinking from the river. I walk over to the child, who looks up at me. The child is crying. The child speaks to me in a language I can't understand, but the words are clearly words of supplication, and the child is looking to me for help and comfort, for assurances for the future. I reach down to pick up the child, but the child is gone. I feel a wave of despair and hope both washing over me. It's going to be all right, I tell the vanished child. It's going to be all right.

Suddenly, I wake up in my bed in my small room at the monastery, breathing in, breathing out.

My wife, Coco, is a dream wizard. As a child she could remember every dream she had, and she's pursued that unique ability all through her life. She was the fourth-ever Westerner to venture into the jungles of northern Malaysia to spend time with the Senoi dream people, a primitive subculture that has lived undisturbed for a very long time. Every morning the entire small tribe would gather together in a circle and share their dreams. The children were taught to run from a tiger in their waking life but to confront it directly in their dreams. If a problem with another tribe member came up in a dream, the dreamer would go to that person and make amends. Before the Malaysian government decided that the Senoi needed to live properly in wood homes raised above the forest floor and embarked on an aid program designed to bring the tribe into the twentieth century, a program that brought illness and dissension instead, there was little, if any, conflict within the Senoi culture.

When she finally arrived with an interpreter at the Senoi's camp, the head of the tribe greeted her warmly, told her that he'd been expecting her for some time, adopted her as his daughter, and began teaching her everything he knew about dreams: how to remember every dream, how to be awake in your dream, how to shift your dream so that, whatever form the frightening tiger takes, you can turn things around so the dream no longer scares you but reveals things you need to know. Humans can lie, but dreams never do.

I love hearing her stories about the time she spent with the Senoi, at least in part because I'm something of a dream dud myself. I rarely recall any dreams at all. I know I have them, but I don't remember them. They fade quickly once I emerge out of sleep. One of the things I love about going on a meditation retreat is that I become far more aware of my dreams.

They're much more vivid, one technicolor episode after the other, and when I wake in the morning, they don't evaporate so quickly. They're still there, and for the most part I can remember them, reenter them, and play them back, as though they'd been recorded on videotape. I'm so grateful for my dream last night. It confirms why I came here to this remote monastery:

> *to bring breath alive*
> *and body awake*
> *so that i might eventually find*
> *that i'm breathing god*
>
> *and to confirm*
> *that it's possible*
> *for all god's children*

Are we all not children of the one God, breathing the same breath? Dismantle the protective scaffoldings that we've erected around ourselves, like the shells of turtles that protect their soft bodies, and aren't we all the same at our soft core, in our essential nature, at the center of our body and mind? Is there a Jewish breath distinct from a Muslim breath different from a Christian breath? Nor are we turtles needing to protect the vulnerabilities of the heart, distinguishing ourselves from one another by the applied shells of our superficial beliefs. When consumed by anger and enmity, which is always and only directed toward another, can you even breathe, let alone be aware of the breath you're taking in, the breath you're letting out? A breath of love is entirely different from a breath of anger or fear. It's full. It's relaxed. It's gentle. It's deep. It radiates warmth and caring, an understanding that everything is connected. It includes the other, inviting the other to join together rather than excluding the other and seeing him or her as different, suspicious, threatening, as other.

> *may peace be with you dear brother*
> *may peace be with you dear sister*
> *peace be with you followers of moses*
> *peace be with you lovers of jesus*
> *peace be with you sons and daughters*
> *   of muhammad*

To heal into God is no small task, and there are many more burdens to drop. But after my time in retreat, I know that it's possible. To resolve the *otherness* with which Christians, Muslims, and Jews all suspiciously view one another, to transform it into a shared and identical experience based on their common heritage, is no small task. But after my time in retreat, I know that it's possible. And that nothing less is necessary.

I remember back to the first day of retreat when everything felt so awkward, and the prospect of bringing breath to awareness and then surrendering to its potency, welcoming the presence of God into my body on an inhalation, seemed like a quixotic idea, a foolish and perhaps far too hubristic endeavor to attempt. But gradually, the days have passed. Breath is more with me now than not. How could I have overlooked it, held it in, run from it?

thoughts are like clouds
that hide the blue sky
of god's presence

clouds come and go
dissolving into brightness

breath comes and goes
dispersing thoughts
entering brightness
like an art restorer
removing layers of veneer
from the surface of a painting
that shows god's face

Guidelines for Going into Retreat

As my son, when he was younger, was fond of saying about pretty much anything I'd do: "If my dad can do this, ANYBODY can do this." When it comes to the practice of Breathing God, he couldn't have been more accurate. I'm no more qualified to take up this practice than anyone else. Like the monks who would sometimes cover their heads to go inside, I constantly wrestle with deep, dark places in my body and mind. If I can do this, anyone can do this. You breathe, don't you? Well, you're a perfect candidate for the practice then. The opening is there whenever you want it. You just have to want it and, I guess, understand why you want it.

Spending otherwise profitable time pursuing the elusive source out of which everything emerges, why would anyone want to do this, why do I want to experience this larger opening, this alternative dimension of reality, why do I want to know about this parallel dimension where things are separate no more and God can be found?

The answer, for me at least, feels simple in this moment: because it feels so very much better there, because it just feels right, because the feeling—and the consciousness that accompanies it—draws me to it like a magnet I can't any longer resist. Riding on the magic carpet of my breath, disappearing through the hidden doorway of my merged feeling presence, visual field, and sounds, even if just for a little minute, heals the pain of separation. Being closer to God feels better.

———◂▸———

Anyone can explore this practice, and you needn't prepare yourself for it in any way. Just set some time aside and start bringing breath to awareness. How much time? It doesn't matter. The honest answer is as much as you can make time for in your busy life. You may want to enter into a retreat of Breathing God for a single day. You may want to start on a Friday evening and finish when you fall asleep on Sunday evening. You may be able to spend a week, ten days, a month, three months breathing in . . . breathing out . . . surrendering . . . in your own way replicating that moment when God blew life into Adam.

Always begin by simply focusing your attention in the felt area of your belly as you watch yourself breathing in and out. You may want to do this for several hours or several days or even weeks. In truth, this is all you need to do. Just breathe, and everything else will happen on its own.

Remember that Breathing God awakens breath and feeling presence both. So remember to feel. Your body. From head to foot a stream of minuscule, wave-like sensations. Feel and breathe, feel and breathe. Your mind will naturally keep taking you away. Don't view that as a problem or evidence that you're somehow not doing the practice right. Just go back to feeling and breathing.

You can recline on your bed, all day long if you like. You may sit in a comfortable chair. You may sit cross-legged on the floor in an Eastern meditation posture. Again, it doesn't matter. Just stay as comfortable as possible and breathe.

Maybe at some point your experience might shift and you feel drawn to start imagining spirit entering your body on your inhalation, sending peace out to the world on your exhalation. Or you find that the *you* in you starts to disappear and the God in you starts to materialize. Or you feel sensation, vision, and sound starting to commingle, merging together on the breath. Or who knows what experiences await you? You may want to explore some of the meditations I've written about in this book. Or you may want to just breathe.

Be open to anything. Don't think that any awareness related to the breath is better, or more advanced, than any other. The longer you breathe, the deeper you naturally go, but the strategy for whatever you're experiencing is the same: let go and breathe and be aware of what happens. So just breathe. You don't have to go searching for experiences. Remember that just breathing is what reveals the hidden mysteries. The goal is simply to be with the breath you're breathing right now, as fully as possible . . . and now the next one. If you just focus on breath, you'll find what you seek.

During your retreat, no matter how long it is, eat lightly.

Take brisk walks. Keep your body clean. Do your best. Know that whatever's happening, you're doing your best. You can't do otherwise.

I don't like saying things such as, "You owe it to yourself." Instead, know that you deserve this. You can do this. Yes, you can. You have all the resources and all the instructions you need. Best wishes on your retreat!

Acknowledgments

Great thanks to my loving wife, Coco, who would listen to every chapter and be my sounding board as to what read well and what needed work, in some cases a lot of work.

Thanks as always go to all the good folks at Inner Traditions who've supported this book, in particular Patricia Rydle, Meghan MacLean, Kate Mueller, Erica Robinson, Ashley Kolesnik, Jeanie Levitan, and Jon Graham.

And special thanks to the Benedictine monks of the Monastery of Christ in the Desert, who welcomed me into their community with open hearts and a calm, mindful presence so I could enter into silent retreat and explore the practice of Breathing God on which this book is based. May peace be with you always and forever.

Index